CW01495039

A Sterne Lent

*Forty Days with the Celebrity Parson the
Church Forgot*

To Catherine,

*Hoping you find value in
this, enjoyment and thank you
for your self today.*

Chris Swift   31-1-25

Q

First Published in Great Britain in 2024

7 Grape Lane, Petergate, York YO1 7HU
Tel: +44 (0)1904 635967
Email: info@quacks.info
Website: radiusonline.info

Quacks Books is an imprint of Radius Publishing Ltd

Copyright © Chris Swift 2024

The moral right of Chris Swift to be identified as the author of
this work has been asserted in accordance with the Copyright,
Designs and Patents Act of 1988.

All rights reserved. No part of this publication may be
reproduced, stored in a retrieval system, or transmitted
in any form or by any means, electronic, mechanical,
photocopying, recording, or otherwise, without the
prior permission of both the copyright owner and the
above publisher of this book.

A CIP catalogue record for this book is
available from the British Library.

ISBN: 978-1-912728-92-3

Set on a page size of 148 x 210mm printed on offset one
hundred gsm chosen for its sustainability.

Chris Swift

Chris Swift is an Anglican priest, spiritual director, theological educator, and author who has worked extensively in health and social care chaplaincy. He is a Visiting Professor at Staffordshire University and a Visiting Fellow at the University of Leeds and has published many book chapters and academic papers. His best-known title is *Hospital Chaplaincy in the Twenty-first Century* published by Routledge. Chris writes regularly on a variety of topics at www.chrisswift.blog.

Cover photograph: the pulpit steps, Sutton-on-the-Forest. According to Pevsner, these early Georgian steps would have been used by Laurence Sterne in accessing the pulpit.

Contents

Key works by Laurence Sterne

9   Foreword

13   Acknowledgements

15   Introduction

25   Lent

39   Week One

59   Week Two

77   Week Three

97   Week Four

117   Week Five

137   Week Six - Holy Week

155   Easter Day

157   Afterword

Key Works by Laurence Sterne

A Political Romance
a satire on church politics in York   *1759*

The Life and Opinions of Tristram Shandy,
Gentleman (in 9 volumes)   *1759 onwards*

A Sentimental Journey Through France and Italy   *1768*

Sermons - individually printed; as part of collections of
sermons; and as individual volumes. There are 42 surviving sermons.

Letters   *1739-1768*

All quotations from Sterne's work are taken from the
Florida Edition.

All quotations from the Bible are from the King James Version.

For Maggie

Foreword

This is a remarkable book and refreshing in its approach to 18th-century life in the Church of England, brought vividly to fruition by Chris Swift's innovative approach to the writings of Laurence Sterne (1713-1768). Most readers will know Sterne through his *The Life and Opinions of Tristram Shandy, Gentleman;* some of the sermons he wrote as an Anglican clergyman, perhaps his *A Sentimental Journey Through France and Italy;* and possibly his less well-known *A Political Romance*. At the time of his death, Sterne was a feted novelist, astute observer of character, and witty cultural commentator. His scathing satirical *Political Romance* infuriated the church when it was published, and most copies were burnt.

Nonetheless, Sterne continued to be the toast of many of the clubs, societies, and meetings that sprung up in British cities during the Age of Enlightenment. Sterne's writing took a po-faced established church down a peg or two. His successors today might include the likes of Fergus Butler-Gallie or perhaps encompass the fictional clergy in TV dramas – the Revd. Geraldine Grainger (Vicar of Dibley) or the hapless Revd. Adam Smallbone (Rev.) come to mind. Sarcasm, or satire, said Oscar Wilde, is the lowest form of wit. I beg to differ. Wit itself is a complex concept. In its original meaning, it implied knowledge, conscience and intelligence. To have wit was 'to know'. To lose your wit – be at your wit's end – was to not know. It was only really in the 17th century that 'wit' became connected to humour, and this is perhaps not surprising when one considers the testing of authority and institutional entitlement that preceded the Enlightenment.

Wit is but one way of reducing the power and estimation of individuals and institutions that think far too much of themselves.

It is also one of the neglected ways of reconnecting with the path of humility in our Lenten journey. Sterne's humour was an essential component in the public recalibration of the Church of England in the 18th century. Pompous, self-regarding, unaccountable and fiscally obese on the revenues from its tithes and glebe, the church and its clergy presented sizeable targets ripe for satire. Sterne duly delivered.

Satire also requires knowledge, deftness and serious acuity. Jesus was no stranger to deploying waspish, scathing wit to prick the consciences of the self-righteous religious leaders of his day, undermining them in front of the very audiences that were usually on the receiving end of stand-offish, elite and smug religiosity.
In the 21st century, the need for religious satire is just as great, and a devotional study of one of its finest exponents is only to be commended. So, I warmly welcome Chris Swift's novel and sage book, especially as a companion in Lent, where we are urged to humble ourselves.

What Chris Swift has given us in this remarkable and refreshing volume is a book for our age. If our pathway through Lent can be illuminated by the likes of Laurence Sterne, we may begin to discover once again that God is, after all, outside the walls of the church, and completely at home in the life of the 'secular'. Turn the pages of this exquisite book, and I wager you will discover exactly that. Lent is all about discovering and cleaving to God in the wilderness we find ourselves in, just as Jesus and John the Baptist did in their own forty days of solitude.

Let Chris Swift's wise and considered book become a cherished spiritual guide for what lies ahead. The journey will be worth it.

The Very Revd Professor Martyn Percy

Provost Theologian, Ming Hua College, Hong Kong;
Professor Religion and Culture, University of St. Joseph, Macao;
Senior Research Associate, The James Hutton Institute, Aberdeen;
Professor Institut für Christkatholische Theologie. Univ. of Bern, CH.

Acknowledgements

There are many people without whom this book would never have been written. I first experimented with the use of Laurence Sterne's work during a York Diocesan Clergy Retreat in October 2023. As I shared some parts of Sterne's preaching and writing it was clear that very few clergy were aware of him and that, secondly, there was enjoyment, fascination and interest in what this unusual vicar was writing 250 years ago. In particular, people seemed unaware that in the arts and humanities Sterne remains a significant influence, continuing to inspire creative responses and artistic developments. It became clear to me that there is an appetite for people to learn more about writing which has such enduring power. I am therefore grateful to those who took part in the retreat, and offered feedback, which encouraged me to pursue the writing of this book.

I have been very fortunate in finding support, resources and encouragement from the curator of the Shandy Hall Museum, Patrick Wildgust and the museum's volunteer co-ordinator, Chris Pearson. At an early stage of writing, I sent a sample of reflections to Chris, and she was kind enough to offer critique and encouragement for the project to progress. I am very grateful to both Patrick and Chris for their interest and support, not to mention the opportunity to sit in Sterne's chair, in Sterne's study, doing a small part of this work.

To a lesser and a greater extent, many people have been very tolerant of my desire to talk about Sterne and his work. I am grateful to the York Minster Library and Archives for providing access to some original material relating to Sterne, and to Martyn Percy for not only offering feedback on an initial sample of the reflections, but for also furnishing the book with both a Foreword and an Afterword that identify and develop some of the underlying theology of the book.

My life-drawing tutor, Rob Oldfield, kindly accepted the challenge to create two drawings in the style of William Hogarth to illustrate the book. In both cases, I believe these are the first drawings ever made of two details from Sterne's work. They add immeasurably to the book, and I cannot thank Rob enough for his interest and enthusiasm for this project.

Two of my longest-standing friends, Mary Leigh and Veronica Hydon, were kind enough to provide feedback, commentary and encouragement at several points during the work and I am thankful for their indulgence of my eccentric interest in Sterne, and even more grateful for our long and continuing friendship.

It is fitting that the publishers of this book, QUACKS - "The Queen Anne Copy Shop" - claim a heritage that goes back to York in the early 17th century. The founder of QUACKS was a friend of Laurence Sterne, and it is quite possible that the first two volumes of *Tristram Shandy* were printed on his presses. The current managing director, Martin Nelson, has been consistently helpful, patient, and affirming. I am grateful to Martin and his team for their advice and suggestions which have undoubtedly improved the content and presentation of *A Sterne Lent*.

Lastly, I am very thankful indeed to the trustees of the Sessions Book Trust, whose generous grant towards the costs of production has enabled this project to come to fruition.

Introduction

A book for Lent drawing on the work of Laurence Sterne might well be called a *"Shandean"* project. Sterne coined the word to describe a slightly skewed and mirthful approach to life, in which humour puts the world into perspective and helps the blood to flow. For that reason, a Sterne Lent can never be an entirely stern season. The 18th century Yorkshire vicar-author was adept at puncturing the pomposities of his time, including his own affectations. In his principal work, *The Life and Opinions of Tristram Shandy, Gentleman* (hereafter, *Tristram Shandy*), Sterne observes with an incisive wit the absurdities of a small world, shaped by its history, disputes, characters and prevailing convictions. If that isn't sufficient reason to turn to Sterne, there's the fact that his first published book - *A Political Romance* - was met with an instruction from the Archbishop of York for all copies to be retrieved and burned. Sadly, this Lent book is unlikely to receive any similar fillip to publicity and the boosted sales of subsequent publications.

Lent books are intended to provide a focus for reflection during the forty days from Ash Wednesday to Easter Day. Sundays, as feast days, are excluded from the calculation. In *A Sterne Lent* these reflections are developed in conversation with the written legacy of Laurence Sterne. There is far more to Sterne's work than a wistful retrospective of a bygone England. In the arts and humanities Sterne continues to generate inspiration and provoke creativity. Almost 250 years after its publication, in 2005, a film of *Tristram Shandy* was made - *A Cock and Bull Story* - with a cast which included Rob Brydon, Steve Coogan and Gillian Anderson. Leading authors still tip their hat to Sterne's achievement and a wandering pen line printed in *Tristram Shandy* has inspired one of London's latest installations of public art.

However, if Sterne's legacy is an active ingredient in the arts, it is a very different story in the Church. His name doesn't darken any date in the Anglican cycle of commemorations - unlike those of Johnson, Donne, Herbert and the Wesley brothers.

Yet Sterne's influence on the world of literature and, consequently, human empathy and understanding, is almost unrivalled. In many lists of the most influential novels of all time, *Tristram Shandy* is present.

Who was Laurence Sterne?

Sterne was a relatively poor member of a family that enjoyed wealth and privilege within the Church of England. However, Sterne's soldier-father was the second son of a second son, and did not have the advantages bought by inheritance. Born in Ireland, Laurence attended school in Halifax, Yorkshire, from the age of 10. Despite the death of his father when he was 17, family connections helped the talented youth to receive a good education and start professional life in the church. He married Elizabeth, and from several pregnancies, only one child lived to become an adult.

After a curacy, with the aid of a clerical relative, Sterne came to serve in churches in north Yorkshire, not far from York. While senior appointments eluded him, other than a position at York Minster, Sterne found in writing an alternative avenue - and revenue - for his talents. His final parish was the living of Coxwold, where his vicarage is today a museum dedicated to his life and work - Shandy Hall. It was in these unremarkable rural parishes that *Tristram Shandy* would be conceived and delivered. Sterne was a cleric of the era, which meant that there were opportunities to subsidise parish income with other roles open to the clergy. The array of pecuniary tasks available was one of the reasons that very heated clerical disputes arose in the 18th century. Sterne secured positions as Commissar from the Dean of York and his patron, Lord Fauconberg. This involved him in presiding over ecclesiastical courts in various villages in the Diocese. It may have been through this work that Sterne was furnished with a detailed knowledge of human behaviour and all its many follies and absurdities.

Sterne was tasked by his uncle, Jacques Sterne (Precentor of York Minster) to take an active part in the religious disputes present in the city. Largely, this consisted of anti-Jacobite narratives published in the local paper, often anonymously. Some of this work spilled over into the many sermons which Laurence preached. This appears to have been the beginning of Sterne's work as a writer.

This limelight-loving cleric discovered a rare talent for innovative writing, which is a defining feature of his publications. His work, most notably *Tristram Shandy*, is joyous and vivid; fantastical and deeply human. In the 18th century it seems remarkable that a Yorkshire vicar could achieve fame through a novel that begins with an account of the principal character's conception. While countless people have loved the twists and turns of a book composed of digressions, for others it has been read as a frustrating, flippant and vacuous piece of prose. Dr Johnson was unimpressed and dismissed it as a passing fad. While writing brought Sterne money to spend it did not accrue the kind of wealth that became the foundation for family dynasties. In 1759 Sterne brought his wife and daughter to live in York, observing in correspondence that, for Lydia, "if I cannot leave her a fortune, I will at least give her an education". Furthermore, by renting a house in Minster Yard, Sterne advanced the possibility of a more significant role in the life of the cathedral: a wish that was to come to nothing.

Laurence Sterne died aged 54. He had rarely enjoyed good health, suffering from tuberculosis, and his trips abroad were made in an effort to improve his condition. Alongside chronic pain, it is certain that his state of health must often have been a considerable struggle. His *Shandean* determination to maintain good spirits and see the lighter side of life would not always have been easy and there is evidence of him suffering despite this desire for good humour.

Was Sterne serious about his faith?

Laurence Sterne was not a saint, if, by that, we mean someone unblemished and beyond reproach. He appears to have been remarkably frank about his sins and omissions. In *A Sentimental Journey*, Sterne implies a forensic attitude towards the temptations of his alter ego, Parson Yorick: "I write not to apologize for the weaknesses of my heart… but to give an account of them". There are questions about Sterne's marital fidelity; a love of fame and fortune; his role as an ecclesiastical judge punishing unmarried mothers; an occasional lapse in clerical duties (distracted by shooting game); and a general lack of ecumenical and inter-faith sympathies. In much of this he was a man of his time.

One of the most popular pamphlets written against Sterne was crafted by a hack masquerading as the first convenor of the Methodist Conference: the preacher George Whitefield. It appeared in the form of a letter to Sterne and went to town on the author of *Tristram Shandy,* accusing him of corruption and writing obscenity. It described *Tristram Shandy* as an anti-gospel, and its author worthy of being called the Antichrist. In particular, it took exception to Sterne's interest in wit and humour, arguing that "mirth is nearly akin to wickedness", and that the "tickling of laughter is occasioned by the obscene devil". Sterne would have been entertained by this satirical huffing and puffing of indignation, and grateful for the publicity. Styled as an attack, recent criticism has suggested that it is in reality a lampoon upon the straightlaced earnestness of early Methodist enthusiasm.

Set against a negative portrayal of Sterne's faith and ethics it is only right to recall comments by Thomas Jefferson, the third President of the USA, who found that Sterne's fiction and sermons constituted: "the best course of morality that ever was written". Jefferson found a kindred spirit in Sterne's writing on conscience and the practical consequences of humanity and compassion. Perhaps more than anyone other writer, Sterne inspired the imagination of the primary author of the USA's Declaration of Independence.

Relevance

There is a story, which cannot be confirmed with certainty, that following his death Sterne's body was exhumed and taken to the University of Cambridge for anatomical study. It is unclear whether this happened in the general business of the "resurrectionist" trade or was a corpse requested in particular. In any event, Sterne was not allowed to rest in peace for very long. In due course his body was recognised by the anatomists and is said to have been returned and reburied. In 1969, due to development taking place on the burial ground at St George Hanover Square, Sterne was once again disinterred and, this time, reburied in the churchyard of his last parish, St Michael Coxwold.

What was true for Sterne's mortal remains also appears to be true for his literary corpus. The reception of his work has never settled on a single interpretation. His legacy has been worked and reworked, inspiring all kinds of developments and novelties. For example, one recent manifestation of this can be found in Orchard

Place, Westminster, where the sculptor Nick Hornby has created a work that reflects Sterne's experimental use of presentation within *Tristram Shandy*. The text is interrupted by a squiggle - a gesture composed of a line that meanders across the page. In 2023 Hornby created this in physical form, expressing a move away from constraint and convention towards freedom. Sterne's legacy will not lie down.

When I mention Sterne to colleagues and people I meet in churches and elsewhere, I am often met with a look of bemusement. If the world of arts and humanities continues to feed on the inspiring work of this Yorkshire parson, it seems that people of religious faith are happy to let him go. As you might imagine, I think this is a mistake. I hope that this Lent book will go some way to address this unfamiliarity with one of the church's most notable clerics. Engaging with Sterne's wit and wisdom can be a rewarding endeavour, and history has a valuable habit of helping us see the present in a fresh light. Given the endless debates and divisions in the Church of England, also known in other churches and religions, a little humour and humanity may go a long way.

Sterne tells us that the "solemn season" of Lent, when abstinence of some form is encouraged, disposes "us for cool and sober reflections" which will:

> Incline us to turn our eyes inwards upon ourselves, and consider what we are, - and what we have been doing; - for what intent we were sent into the world, and what kind of characters we were designed to act in it.

Sterne understood Lent to be a time to "call home the conscience". Yet he is anxious to avoid any sense that deprivation should feed some kind of inner thirst for the denial of pleasure. Sterne is conscious of the weaknesses of human nature and the temptations of excess. He addresses the question as to how we strike the right balance - between indulgence and denial. Intriguingly, Sterne employs a metaphor which is a memorable feature of his opening chapter of *Tristram Shandy*. In this chapter Tristram's conception occurs on the first Sunday of the month, the day when it was his father's habit to bring together various domestic duties, of which winding up the clock was but one. In his sermon entitled "Penances", he argues that human beings know intuitively where the boundaries of conscience lie and that we have not been sent into the world "on purpose to go mourning, all our lives long, in sack-cloth and ashes". We know that pleasure is needed to refresh our souls and bodies "which, like clocks, must be wound up at certain intervals".

A Personal Conversation

I am writing this book after more than thirty years of ordained ministry. I am several years older than the age Sterne had attained by the time of his death. Most of my ministry has been in health and social care chaplaincy. My interest in Sterne goes back to my undergraduate days at the University of Hull, studying Theology and English Literature. My copy of *Tristram Shandy* from the mid-1980s is annotated and well-thumbed. I've no idea what, if any, essays arose from this study, but my reading inspired an enduring fascination with this unusual author and priest.

Moving to York in 2019, I found myself often passing the plaque dedicated to Jacque Sterne, Laurence's uncle and one-time Precentor of York Minster. Each time I enter the Minster on the north side I pass the funerary statue of his great-grandfather, Archbishop Richard Sterne. From time to time, I have conducted services in churches with a Sterne connection, in one way or another.

My fascination with his writing and ministry grew as I visited his former Rectory, now the museum dedicated to furthering the appreciation and understanding of his work. For the first time, I read his sermons and wondered about the complex figure who preached the Christian religion and portrayed the characters of his age with such warmth, humanity, insight and wit.

I do not pretend that the scholarship underpinning these reflections for Lent adds very much to the critical analysis which has been undertaken by academics specialising in this field. However, I come to Sterne's work as a contemporary cleric and bring to his life and works a spirit that continues to wrestle with the meaning of God's purpose for the world, holding in creative tension and dialogue both the secular and the sacred. As an Anglican, I am committed to the dynamic relationship of scripture, tradition, and reason. As a theologian in the liberal tradition, I recognise some inheritance from the late Latitudinarians to whom Sterne belonged, and the value of a thoughtful middle ground in matters of religion.

It is well established that Sterne would purloin phrases and ideas from other preachers and writers. This is not always credited, and it cannot be asserted that all he wrote or preached was unique. Despite many anachronisms and prejudices of his time, there are words, phrases and ideas that reach across the centuries and remind us that many of our challenges in faith and life are neither new nor novel. In his lampooning of nascent medical technology and its impact on religion, Sterne's work presses home the need for wit and a sense of proportion to temper the eagerness of human progress.

Approach

A Sterne Lent consists of 40 reflections arising from my own experiences and perspectives, in conversation with the legacy of Laurence Sterne. Although designed for the season of Lent they may be read in any way, at any time. I have endeavoured to avoid imposing any particular pattern on the reflections, although it will be apparent that some themes recur and develop across the six weeks. The engagement with Sterne's work is inevitably selective and provides the impetus for thoughts that resonate across the years. While the location of writing - the city of York - offers a hint of continuity, the scope of change across almost every aspect of social, political and religious life is evident at every turn.

Indeed, some readers have found Sterne's endless digressions frustrating. In one of his better-known quotations from *Tristram Shandy*, he stated that these "incontestably, are the sunshine;—they are the life, the soul of reading;—take them out of this book for instance,—you might as well take the book along with them". I hope this provides ample justification for the structure of a Lent book which, in its forty episodes, is a journey through many unconnected reflections and incidents. However, in the telling, there are also instructive detours, and emerging themes, which still have the power to surprise.

At ordination, I was part of a small group of fellow travellers undertaking the absurd journey of ministry, with its towering expectations and seemingly limitless responsibilities. One of this cell group arranged for a calligrapher to design some words from the poetry of TS Eliot to frame and hang in a suitable place.

"We shall not cease from exploration
And the end of all our exploring
Will be to arrive where we started
And know the place for the first time".

TS Eliot, *Little Gidding*

As I sit at my desk, and look to the left, these words are there. The exploration never ends so long as we are alive, and time has a great ability to alter what we once knew so well.

Laurence Sterne has made me laugh. At times I can feel the sentiment of his obvious shortcomings and peccadillos. I never doubt his humanity or, come to that, his basic desire to live in a world that might be more peaceful; hopeful; and mirthful.

It is my hope that this book will introduce Laurence Sterne to new readers and demonstrate that his literary legacy continues to epitomise and stimulate a lively, witty, compassionate and thoughtful faith. Although his writing and life have generated controversy, and this will no doubt continue to be the case, it would be foolish to ignore Sterne solely for this reason. The unusual gaze of this country parson, combined with candour and self-deprecation, make him a good companion amidst the uncertainties and dangers of our own time, and a church inclined to take itself far too seriously, and not seriously enough. In digressions and the juxtaposition of events lies the sunshine that is the sole remedy for what could otherwise be, as Sterne put it, "one cold eternal winter". At the end of this journey, it will be for the reader to decide whether they have spent forty days in the company of the Antichrist - or six weeks coming to know a flawed genius who exemplified exceptional empathy, faith, wit and compassion.

Lent

1. Ash Wednesday

The First Hour of Wisdom

On Ash Wednesday the theme of return to God pervades the readings and prayers of the Church. In many instances, clergy will offer the "Imposition of Ashes" - a sign made on the forehead using the charred remains of last year's palm crosses. The act is accompanied by words that name our mortality with unadorned simplicity: "Remember that you are but dust".

The themes of loss and return define the parable of the Prodigal Son. In Sterne's sermon on the story from Luke 15, he wonders about the many implications of the parable where "the story is silent - but nature is not". Did the father attempt to dissuade the younger son? Did the family plead with him to abandon his plan to leave home with the sum total of his inheritance? Alas, as Sterne reflects, "the dissuasive would but inflame his desire". It is characteristic of our first taste of independence to act in direct opposition to well-intentioned parental advice. In the case of the Prodigal, the parent lets go of the child who leaves the shelter of home to go "forth into a storm".

Many times during my ministry I have been asked about the apparent absence of God during the personal storms we encounter, or when people despair of the world. When things are not as we would wish them to be, it is tempting to assign responsibility to a God who appears unwilling to act. Yet Good Friday reminds us that even when suffering touched God most directly, there was no magical moment of salvation from pain.

Suffering should never be glorified, but there are sometimes lessons to draw when we find ourselves in its midst. As Sterne identifies, in the Gospel account we hear nothing about the Prodigal's concern for his father while there is money to spend and new experiences to hazard. In this case, hardship dispels an illusion and engenders sobriety:

> His first hour of distress, seem'd to be his first hour of wisdom.

Being reminded of our mortality is seldom comfortable. It is a great strength of religion that it holds us to the truth of our finite nature. As a hospital chaplain, I learned how the impending end of life, in situations where an emergency marriage was required, altered how I heard the liturgy. Usually at a wedding service, the references to death can feel innocuous and far distant - almost unheard. However, when one of the parties has but a short time to live, these words acquire a sudden weight. In such circumstances the likelihood of death's proximity lifts the words from the page - but they are always there, and always name the fundamental nature of our being.

Sterne suggests that human beings are often highly resistant to stories of wisdom when delivered as a straightforward lesson. To be effective they must have "the groundwork of a story which engages the passions". Maybe, as he suggests in the sermon, this is because "like iron" we "must first be heated before we can be wrought upon". Alternatively, perhaps our hearts are so in love with deceit that we need a fable to cheat our perception into grasping the truth.

> But when he was yet a great way off, his father saw him, and had compassion, and ran, and fell on his neck, and kissed him. And the son said unto him, Father, I have sinned against heaven, and in thy sight, and am no more worthy to be called thy son. But the father said to his servants,

Bring forth the best robe, and put it on him; and put a ring on his hand, and shoes on his feet: And bring hither the fatted calf, and kill it; and let us eat, and be merry: For this my son was dead, and is alive again; he was lost, and is found. And they began to be merry.

Luke 15: 20b-24

The stoical elder son stays outside this celebration. Once again, the parent moves towards the child, seeking reconciliation and joy. The wisdom of love and age waits upon youth. Inside, the celebration is already underway, where gentle spirits "light up the pavilion with a sacred fire; and parental love, and filial piety lead in mask with riot and festivity!" Such humanity, compassion, forgiveness and joy are meat and drink to the preacher. The candour of the younger son, and his misadventures in the world, resonate with the life of Laurence Sterne. Perhaps this pavilioned party is an image of heaven that stirs his heart? The joy-without-judgement of finding what was lost; the embrace of unqualified love for what was dead and is now alive.

Ash Wednesday can feel like unlooked-for gloom. A day to flee, and a theme to dull. We don't like to recall that we are but dust, and to dust we shall return. Thankfully, the Christian hope is that while our life on earth may end, there is one who longs with perfect love to welcome us home. To forgive us all that is past. Not a figure who waits in scowling judgement for us to list our many failings and follies, but a joyous love that reaches out to us while we are still far off. A love that runs to heal in one embrace all that has gone amiss, and to rejoice in our return. What is the consequence of dust in the face of such a meeting?

2. Thursday

The World Undone or A Fair and Guarded Outside

> So full are our minds of other matters, that we have not time to ask, or a heart to answer the questions we ought to put to ourselves.

Many of us will be familiar with the challenges posed by the task of self-reflection. We are the self doing the reflecting, and when there are errors or distortions in our sight it may be almost impossible for us to see what is obvious to others. This challenge is addressed by Sterne in one of his sermons. He notes the temptation we may all encounter when we turn enquiry into apology:

> Whose business is not to search for the truth, but skilfully to hide it.

Sterne shrewdly identifies the temptation we may all encounter during self-examination, of looking around us rather than within us. In other words, that we excuse, justify or temper our bad behaviour by finding someone more malicious or proud, and make them the measure of our conduct. Sterne finds a biblical example of this in the parable of the Pharisee and the publican (Luke 18: 9-14). The first thoughts of the former, on entering the synagogue, are to make a flattering comparison with the life of the latter. In a manner that speaks to our own time with equal force, Sterne argues that the sins of the Pharisee are different, but in essence, made of the same stuff. Perhaps, Sterne wonders, the Pharisee used religion as a cloak for ambition and worldly motives?

This sermon holds a particular fascination concerning Sterne's own conduct. There is plenty of evidence that he was not faithful, in one sense or another, to his wife. An interview with someone who had been in his service recalled visits to York in which the servant was tasked with procuring female company for Sterne. At the same time, given that other details in the servant's account are known to be erroneous, it is unfair to give this unquestioning credence. As we know, Sterne was a complex character and there are legitimate questions about the way he lived and how he fulfilled his role as a parson. Perhaps this sermon offers some kind of insight into how he handled his own reflection upon his conduct. Of the Pharisee:

> If he, lastly, is debauched or intemperate, am I not conscious of as corrupt and wanton dispositions; and that a fair and guarded outside is my best pretence to an opposite Character?

We are left with the question as to whether Sterne should be admired for an openness about the shortcomings of his behaviour, or decried for not cloaking this so well as others? Either way, this sermon appears to show that he was able to model in the act of preaching the kind of reflection which he is arguing for in the text. To quote Shakespeare, perhaps Sterne was, at times, a "plain dealing villain".

Reflecting on the conundrum of conduct and intent, Sterne says that someone may be unalloyed by evil as far as the world is concerned, and "through deep-laid policy and design" deceive the public. Similarly, he argues that when people are suspicious of the "coin" of a benefactor, they will still see if that currency of repute can be traded and whether anyone else will notice. In other words, people may be incurious about someone they have reason to believe is not what they seem, if it is in their interests to play along with the fiction. Here Sterne is drawing on the language of commerce to make his point. The world "gives credit" to people who are generous and do charitable work. People tend not to question the motives of such philanthropists or bring the coin of reputation to any kind of balance to check its authenticity. Reading this in an age that has witnessed so many ostensibly generous people use their status to perpetrate terrible crimes, Sterne's sermon remains remarkably relevant.

Having observed the many pitfalls of serious and beneficial reflection, Sterne concludes that an "honest head, willing to reform itself" is the best hope for our improvement. This will feel too solitary for some, but it reflects Sterne's conviction that little can help us unless we first have the desire and capacity to recognise our own need for change. He asks his hearers to think how easily they observe and weigh the behaviour of others, and to direct that same "critical exactness and same piercing curiosity" to their own conduct. Scripture provides the stipulation of our need for self-reflection, but for Sterne, reason is the application of the rule.

Nothing should be varnished - we must look into the "dark corners and recesses" of our hearts without fear. However, Sterne recognises the power of our self-deception and the tendency we may all find to emulate the Pharisee and deem our faults to be inconsequential when compared to those of others. The risk of collusion is always present, and the task of recognising what lies behind a "fair and guarded outside" is a responsibility about which we can never be complacent.

In every age, there is a need to be cautious about those who appear to be too good to be true. For whatever reason, although he aspired to literary fame, Sterne never invested much effort into constructing a virtuous facade. As we enter into the forty days of Lent it is wise to recognise that our pride dwells in our imagination - not our reality - and that seeing this attractive deception for what it is, naming it and dismantling it, is one of the great obligations of the Christian faith.

> He hath shewed strength with his arm; he hath scattered the proud in the imagination of their hearts.
> He hath put down the mighty from their seats, and exalted them of low degree.
> He hath filled the hungry with good things; and the rich he hath sent empty away.

> Luke 1: 51-53

3. Friday

Fugacious Pleasures

Language is a remarkable thing and the capacity of English to pilfer, absorb and borrow from other languages is, perhaps, its defining feature. Many expressions have fallen into disuse and some words used in the 18th century might leave most of us scratching our heads today. Sterne's reference to fugacious pleasures simply means that these were fleeting experiences, incapable of being pinned down and retained. It is a term used in a Lenten sermon exploring a statement found in Ecclesiastes 7:2:

> It is better to go to the house of mourning, than to the house of feasting…

Sterne was not averse to feasting, or the kind of life that came with the status of being a celebrity (even in the 18th century). In rejecting this aphorism, he questions whether the struggles we face are so few that we "must sally forth in quest of them". For Sterne, it makes no sense that the "Best of Beings" would want humanity to close its eyes to the beauties and benefits that arise during our journey through the world. This can be done, he says, without "forgetting the main errand we are sent upon".

In his sermon entitled "Penances", Sterne pursues the argument that God provides us with both pleasures in life and the means to enjoy those pleasures. Our senses are there so that we may delight, to some degree, in the journey we make through life. This journey comes with "many shocks and hard jostlings", but we should not think that these less pleasant experiences are to be sought out or encouraged. Sterne perceives that the people who frown upon pleasure, or see it as being at odds with religion, do so because they are "conceiving the Deity to be like themselves, a gloomy, discontented and sorrowful being".

There is always the risk that we imagine a God who is a version of ourselves writ large. One of the strongest arguments of religion is when we find that we discern a God who is very different from our own sympathies and inclinations. When we are content that life is proceeding happily in one direction only to feel ourselves called and compelled to travel on a different road. The unresolved ambiguities of Sterne lie to some extent in the degree to which his fictional characters are autobiographical. For example, in *A Sentimental Journey*, Parson Yorick is reprimanded by a hotel manager in Paris because the parson was visited by a chambermaid in the evening. The *maitre d'hotel* comments that this would not have been a concern had it been "in the morning". Yorick asks in reply: "does the difference of the time of day at Paris make a difference to the sin?" Apparently, it did. While there is suggestiveness in the text, there is no direct evidence that Parson Yorick has behaved badly. It then transpires that the hotel manager has fewer objections if a man is visited by a woman who is selling laces etc., and doing so while authorised by the hotel. In other words, it ceases to be a moral issue when the manager has received his cut from the transaction. Yorick's sin, it would seem, was an offence against controlled trade and not the trade itself.

Sterne clearly enjoyed the beauty of people and places and found entertainment in the amiable but often myopic characters he portrayed in his fiction. These were not *bad* people but people who rode their own particular hobby horses and enjoyed whatever fleeting pleasures came their way - not least in friendship, familial affection, and the everyday absurdities of humanity. Perhaps for this reason, Lent for Sterne only had meaning in the purpose to which it pointed, not as denial for denial's sake.

4. Saturday

Mire and Filth

In his sermons, as a parson, and as an ecclesiastical judge, Sterne was concerned with vice. There are several issues arising from this that preoccupy Sterne. For example, why was there still so much vice in Christendom when the Christian faith had been promoted for such a long time? Given the turn to practical divinity stimulated by Puritanism, the question of religion's impact on society was a pressing concern. In his fictional works, Sterne demonstrates his awareness and sensitivity to the criticisms levelled at the clergy. In the chapter of *Tristram Shandy* dealing with the unfortunate Le Fever, an ailing soldier, Corporal Trim expresses his own views about the prayerfulness of two very different professions, clerical and the military:

> … when a soldier gets time to pray, - he prays as heartily as a parson, - though not with all his fuss and hypocrisy.

Corporal Trim is censured for expressing this opinion, not because it is necessarily wrong, but because it is only on the day of judgement that our actions will be reviewed and known. This highlights a conviction shared by Sterne in his sermons and other writing that an excessive show of religion was not a wise idea. Nevertheless, Trim probably expresses a popular view that there are moments in life when the ceremony of religion feels less authentic than the prayer offered in extremis. Perhaps this reinforces a sense that Sterne is deeply interested in our humanity, brought into view by those moments when we cease to pretend that we can wholly control the circumstances in which we find ourselves.

As a commissar for an ecclesiastical court, Sterne sat in judgement on a range of moral violations. It is hard to imagine the degree of fear and distress that the existence of the courts must have caused. St Mary's Alne in North Yorkshire is a picturesque church with parts dating back to the 12th century. It has all the character of ancient English churches that have settled into their ground, with few perpendicular lines that match. The interior shows the signs of great effort and faithful care to preserve a building whose cost of replacement would probably amount to the combined value of all the other buildings in the village. During a recent visit to lead a Sunday service of Holy Communion, I began the sermon by saying that I had been greatly shocked to read about all the immoral behaviour committed by the parishioners of the parish. I added, not far into the address, that the one mitigating factor was that the events described took place in 1751 when Laurence Sterne presided over an ecclesiastical court in the church. As the introduction to a sermon, I have rarely enjoyed such spellbound attention from a congregation.

These courts were shabby affairs, by any standard. They heard evidence concerning cases of fornication; the negligence of church wardens; and anything else touching on the authority of the church or public morality. The reason why fornication was central to proceedings lay in the procreation of children and subsequent costs to the parish. A child without any means of support became a charge upon the finances of the community and, consequently, considerable pressure was brought to bear to name the father. The outcome of a successful prosecution forced the woman, dressed in a white sheet, to come to church on a Sunday, stand on a chair, and make a humiliating confession during the service. Additionally, a fine was imposed, and possibly, a marriage contracted as a "knobstick" wedding. The latter was named in reference to the churchwardens' staves, often topped with a weighty symbol (the knob) and used to coerce a reluctant groom or bride to the altar. It might be described as an early version of the shotgun wedding.

Sterne accepted a central role in these proceedings and no doubt heard much about the life of the community which would not necessarily reach the ears of a vicar today. How we live within imperfect systems and seek to play some small part in redeeming them is a perennial question. On one occasion Sterne sent a note with "a poor woman" who had been fined by a court, telling the officer to whom she went to pay that she was "as poor as a Church Mouse" and offered to pay the fine on her behalf.

Week One

5. Monday

"Get your preferment first, Lory"

I am writing *A Sterne Lent* sitting in a room of a house built around the year 1727 by William Ward. The celebrated Great East Window of York Minster lies a few yards to my right and high up, looking out over the city, is a statue of St Peter, patron of the Metropolitical Cathedral. The Rev. Dr. William Ward was an ecclesiastical lawyer to the Dean and Chapter and made a good living out of the fees and charges associated with this prestigious role. Some evidence of this can be found in his Last Will and Testament, where, along with bequests to his wife and children, he grants £100 (approaching £30,000 in today's value) to a faithful servant. The townhouse sits in Minster Yard, where Sterne would subsequently lease a property. Ward's death in 1751 was the pebble that fell into a pool of clerical ambition and led Laurence Sterne to become a novelist.

With Ward's death, all his ecclesiastical and legal duties were up for grabs. The Archbishop's chief legal officer - Dr Topham - believed two of these had been promised to him by the Dean. The Dean either thought he hadn't made any such commitment, or he reneged. In either case, the legal officer was furious at this alleged breach of promise. A spat began between these two senior diocesan figures which became public and lasted a decade. It came to an end when Sterne wrote an explosive satire, his first creative piece of writing: *A Political Romance.*

Lampooning the various dimensions of this unholy row about roles, Sterne mocked Dr Topham as the greedy acquisitor of any paid job that was going. Shrinking the drama from a diocesan to a parochial affair, Sterne portrays Topham as the parish Sexton.

Furthermore, in addition to this role, he becomes: dog-whipper; winder and maintainer of the church clock; bailiff; mole-catcher; and also secures for his wife the paid work of washing and darning the church linen. This litany of curious and varied occupations sets the mob laughing. Years later a more mature Sterne would reflect and regret that Dr Topham was the subject of such ridicule. Nevertheless, the satire ended the longstanding dispute between these senior diocesan clerics.

In correspondence with friends, it is clear that those close to Sterne were concerned about his foray into creative writing. As the publication date of *Tristram Shandy* approached, those who had been privileged to see the evolving material urged caution. Some thought the writing would damage his prospects in the church. In reply, Sterne argued that he had tempered the work as much as he could but was concerned that any further changes would spoil its "air and originality". He had no doubt about the "folly of an attempt of castrating my book to the prudish humour of particulars". Also, in terms of advancement, "for aught I know, I may not be preferred till the resurrection of the just".

I wonder over the centuries how many original thoughts and potent truths have been suppressed by the prospect of preferment? I have known a bishop say that some clergy have been so eager to get a "hat" (mitre) that they have been entirely incurious about what being a bishop entails. In becoming an assistant prelate, they failed to ask about the expectations of their new diocesan bishop or how that bishop envisaged the working relationship. It has often led to much angst and disappointment. Prospects - as they used to be called - have a great tendency to engineer conformity of mind and spirit. When someone reaches the age at which they suspect none of these hopes will be realised, there may be a sobering moment when they tally up what they have sacrificed for the sake of nothing.

It appears that Sterne was incapable of holding his peace, even if it would come to cost him advancement. He is somewhat battered and bruised by the church and what he sees as his unrecognised efforts in aiding some of the senior clergy. Satire and mirth bubble out of the Coxwold cleric, and he cannot bear to censure the originality of his work. What friends suggest he remove, he argues, are the very things that make his writing distinctive and new.

At the Archbishop's instruction, his first publication was withdrawn and burned. At least six copies survived the conflagration. However, the experience convinced Sterne that he had a skill that could be both effective and rewarding. The response of the Archbishop created a reputation and an audience. Sterne's commitment to portray his characters with humanity and compassion, eccentricity and vitality, produced a legacy far more enduring than any path to high office.

6. Tuesday

The Mechanics of Faith

In the turmoil of the 18th century, as materialistic philosophies began to have increasing influence, the foundations of the Industrial Revolution were being laid. Sterne was involved in changes which would leave an enduring legacy and alter the relationships of rural communities across England. He supported enclosures and the loss of some common rights which belonged to the wider community. As we shall see across these reflections, Sterne is enmeshed in many of the prevailing behaviours of his class, and he exhibits the prejudices and expectations of a man seeking greater recognition. By supporting enclosure, he was siding with the wealthy and influential figures in his parishes. At the same time, in his satirical writing, he exposed many of the absurdities of the systems and culture of which he was a part.

Several decades ago, I wrote a revue for a conference of the clergy of the Diocese of St Albans. In it, I lampooned the bishop, who had given a speech to the synod in which he reflected on a journey made on London's Underground, where he noted the many pieces of information, advertising, and warnings that littered the carriage. In the revue this became a sermon in which I imagined the bishop on a journey on the Circle Line, where the train passed a station without stopping:

> I imagined what it would be like to take a journey on the Circle Line, when for some reason the train never stopped. Round and round it would go; on a journey that never ended; out of sight of the world and utterly devoid of meaning. And in an instant, I was moved to prayer as I thought of the careers of so many clergy in the Diocese...

To his credit the bishop appeared to take this in good heart (at least that was my interpretation of the first words he said to me after I came off stage: "Right, that's it!").

For all his inevitable complicity, Sterne believed life was about more than being trapped in the mechanics of a journey we neither understood nor controlled. In France he spent several months with a group of philosophers who were unambiguously materialist in their understanding of life. He came to be on first-name terms with David Hume and many other leading exponents of atheism and materialism. As he progressed his final project, *A Sentimental Journey*, he acknowledged the friendship and support of these luminaries even whilst he affirmed his own convictions that sentiment and religious faith were essential parts of our reality.

In *A Sentimental Journey* we meet someone already mentioned in Sterne's earlier work. This is Maria, a bereaved and distracted shepherdess who stirs a profound sympathy in the heart of Sterne's central character, Parson Yorick. The sympathies of the cleric go out to Maria in a description rich in scriptural allusions and redolent of eucharistic reconciliation. Yorick says:

> I have a cottage, I would take thee to it and shelter thee: thou shouldst eat of my bread, and drink of my own cup… in all thy weaknesses and wanderings I would seek thee and bring thee back.

Sterne attempted to convey the sense of empathy and connection, sometimes bound up with eroticism and sexual desire, that stirs human beings into a state of feeling which exceeded a purely mechanical response. In his novels, letters and sermons, this *Shandean* conviction is found time and again. Despite the very warm friendships that he established with the French and British materialists, Sterne could never subscribe to their philosophy. The muddling eccentricities of human behaviour; the reception of the Prodigal by his father; and the love which Sterne experienced in his one life, would not allow the mechanism of a clock (no matter how well-wound) to ration out the mirth that animated his spirit. For Sterne, life may seem perplexing and uncertain, but his conviction is that we are "curiously wrought by an all-wise hand" and in faith we are equipped with hope to both meet our adversity and seek its remedy.

At the end of *A Sentimental Journey* Sterne expresses this firm conviction with a single sentence:

> I am positive I have a soul; nor can all the books with which materialists have pester'd the world ever convince me of the contrary.

7. Wednesday

A Flap upon the Heart

Sterne once sent a letter to the governor of London's Foundling Hospital, accompanying a copy of one of his sermons, which he hoped would serve as a "flap upon the heart". This term is a reference to the third journey made by Gulliver in Jonathan Swift's account of his travels. Gulliver encounters the practice among the better off to have a servant nearby holding an inflated bladder on a stick. From time to time, when it was perceived that the servant's master - or mistress - had become self-absorbed and inattentive, the bladder would be used to "flap" the eyes and ears. This was done gently to aid a full return of concentration. Perhaps it might be described as the 18th century's prototype for mindfulness.

Swift undoubtedly saw the link between the Lilliputian flappers and the ancient custom of court jesters, many of whom carried similarly inflated bladders as part of their performance. In both cases, through a gentle flap, the Fool might alert his master to a truth anyone else would be afraid to utter. Awakening the audience to their reality is the primary purpose.

In this case, Sterne's sermon was intended to flap the consciences of those who would hear it or read it. As can be seen on several occasions, Sterne was sought-after as a preacher for charitable services due to his effectiveness in connecting with congregations and opening the valves of their generosity. With a State which provided very limited means of care and support, charitable endeavours were essential if the least advantaged in society were to survive. As Sterne notes in one of his sermons, this was not a straightforward enterprise and a scoundrel could buy reputation with donations which made little difference to his own material circumstances. The politics of giving are complicated, but at least with charity sermons the donated monies were aggregated rather than individually attributed.

Churches had an important role to play in the anonymisation of giving and fostering a sense of collective responsibility where each could give according to their means. Personal philanthropy conducted in public has a horrible habit of corrupting everyone involved. When two elderly choir members gave a piece of church furniture in memory of their father it was fascinating to observe how much fuss was created if the said item was moved so much as an inch one way or t'other. Over time I came to wonder whether this had been truly given or simply loaned. The attitude of the sisters appeared to be quite proprietary. We are all very bad at making a genuine gift, free from all expectations of gratitude or preferential rights. It is why Good Friday should put to shame any pride we have in our giving. Here, on the cross, God does not exercise any privileged authority over the Word become flesh. A gift is a gift. If, in any sense, it continues to be ours - or we retain preferential influence - it ceases to be a genuine gift.

All of Lent, and especially Holy Week, can be a flap upon the heart. If the world has become staid for us, or our compassion has worn thin in the face of humanity's ubiquitous suffering, these days in the Christian calendar call us to walk in uncomfortable shoes. To take Sterne's point a step further, the flap to the heart we need most is the resuscitation of our humanity and the rekindled desire for a world infused with very different values. In every age, and every religion, we need the jester who will flap our eyes to pay attention to the realities around us and to stir the spirit of true generosity and meaningful compassion.

"A Flap upon the Heart" by Rob Oldfield (reflection 7)

8. Thursday

We Are Deceived

Early in my ministry, I made regular visits to a young man who
was confined to his bed following an accident. His family provided
loving care while also valuing contact and support from the local
church and community. On one occasion I was in the sitting
room where his mother was watching the news. She commented
in passing - following some report of vicious conduct - that she
couldn't pass judgement on the perpetrator of a crime she felt no
temptation to commit. However, on the whole, people are quick
to judge the conduct they have no personal inclination to commit.
Sterne observed that we respond to sins with a "different degree of
detestation" depending on the strength of likelihood we might feel
to perform them.

Lent begins with a sombre recognition of both our mortal nature and
our capacity to sin. "If we say we have no sin, we deceive ourselves,
and the truth is not in us". Or, to put it another way, human beings
have a tendency to avoid uncomfortable truths about themselves
whilst eagerly pontificating on the vices of others. Perhaps, when
we come down to it, the attraction is that the latter provides both
comfort and obscurity to the former.

Remarkably, in recent decades the church has articulated a very
distorted theology of sin. The abuses of powerful figures were
ignored in the past because "a bishop wouldn't do that". It has taken
the courage and witness of survivors and their supporters to break
in upon the myopia of the institution and call people to account.
Even this has come at a personal cost. Yet all the senior figures of
the church who know their Scripture well will be familiar with St
Paul's warning that "even Satan disguises himself as an angel of

light". Elite clubs, possibly even a bench of bishops, demonstrate a notable power to strive for self-preservation.

More than once, Sterne reflects upon human deception in his writing. In his sermon on self-knowledge, he takes the example of King David and Nathan's parable of the rich man who takes a poor man's beloved lamb (2 Samuel 12.7). By drawing on this parable of a stolen lamb, Sterne illustrates the skill needed to provoke us into an accurate estimate of our failings.

This sermon draws from both Dean Swift and Joseph Butler. As human knowledge grew and developed, our everyday failure to understand our own actions clearly caused many 18th-century thinkers some concern. In the story of Nathan and David, Sterne suggests that perhaps the most effective way to counter our blindness to aspects of our own lives is to use a technique that deceives our deception. An effective parable enables us to identify ourselves within a story in ways that may disarm the distortions which would typically hide a course of action from our view. Sterne argues that King David was utterly oblivious to the moral weight of his transgression until the moment Nathan said: "you are the man".

Sterne's attention to the folly and failure of human nature includes a critique of our judgement about vices to which we feel no temptation. He argues that when sin tallies with our desire, we become oblivious to its nature and consequences. Where there is a vice to which we are not addicted, we pass judgement with easy conviction in our moral superiority.

> Thus we are nice in grains and scruples - but knaves in matters of a pound weight - every day straining at gnats, yet swallowing camels - miserably cheating ourselves, and

torturing our reason to bring us in such a report of the sin as suits the present appetite and inclination.

Sterne's response to this reality of human nature is to encourage greater priority for the task of careful reflection. That we should interrupt the regular flow of our behaviour and make time to interrogate our actions. He stresses the importance of "retiring unto ourselves, and searching into the dark corners and recesses of the heart, and taking notice of what passes there". For Sterne, this inner landscape of desire and misperception is labyrinthine, but he remains confident that with sober judgement we can trace the error of our ways.

Recognising our capacity for self-deception is neither easy nor attractive. Perhaps, with discipline and determination, we can use reflective space to recognise the behaviours of which we know we should be ashamed. However, it may be a more fruitful process to do this with a spiritual companion or director. If Sterne is right, the realisation of our vices can be overpowering and shattering - as it was for King David. It is also, if handled constructively, a moment to deepen our relationship with God, to learn and to grow in spiritual maturity.

9. Friday

Tinsel'd Over

Preaching was a big deal in the 18th century. A good thirty-minute sermon was expected, and various charitable endowments would pay for sermons to be given on auspicious days, such as the anniversary of the execution of King Charles I. People would travel some distance to hear a Wesley or sit at the feet of an orator at the top of their game. Queues formed when a bookshop had a new and much-anticipated collection of sermons to sell. Why wait for the latest edition of a favourite novel when you could have *The Abuses of Conscience* hot off the press?

In *Tristram Shandy,* Sterne's alter ego, Parson Yorick, is moved in one chapter to express with some passion his views about the purpose of preaching, and how it should be done.

> To preach, to shew the extent of our reading, or the subtleties of our wit—to parade in the eyes of the vulgar with the beggarly accounts of a little learning, tinsel'd over with a few words which glitter, but convey little light and less warmth——is a dishonest use of the poor single half hour in a week which is put into our hands—'Tis not preaching the gospel—but ourselves——For my own part, continued Yorick, I had rather direct five words point-blank to the heart.—

Yorick is halted in his tracks by an exclamation which, in the style of Sterne, is farcical and has nothing to do with the subject under discussion. A hot chestnut drops by accident between the trouser buttons of one of the men present, creating an effect that graduates from pleasure to pain and then alarm. Little wonder that the word which interrupts Yorick is "Zounds!"

"Zounds" is a contraction of "God's wounds", referring to the crucifixion. Many now redundant expletives were associated with the final hours of the life of Jesus. 'Gadzooks' comes from 'God's hooks', indicating the metal used to secure Christ to the cross. It is a reminder, in one way or another, of how much language and everyday expression contained references to the central events of the Christian faith.

Swearing in Georgian England was not only a concern because of the sensitivities of those present - it could also cost you money. The Profane Oaths Act of 1745 had to be read in Church four times a year and infringing the Act led to fines. If a profanity was made in front of a justice of the peace (many of whom were clergy) no further evidence was required to support the charge. It was only repealed in England in 1967. I wonder, when I have been on hospital wards wearing a clerical collar, and someone nearby swears and instantly apologises, whether this is solely a reflex of politeness, or springs from some deeply buried collective memory of punishment?

Yet this may not be to the point. Yorick is heated by his disappointment about how the unique opportunity to preach the Gospel for half an hour each week was wasted by so many preachers. It may have been a familiar topic for Yorick. Although the phrase "old chestnut" means a stale saying, or an oft-ridden hobbyhorse, it cannot be certain that any link is intended between Yorick's rousing discourse and the chestnut incident: neither can it be disproved. In any event, the misuse of preaching is something that stirs Yorick into a passion. He argues that it should not be to parade the preacher's supposed knowledge or wit before a captive audience. Nor can a sprinkling of glitter transform such excrement into something that offers light and warmth. The latter implies that Yorick understood the purpose of preaching as providing both guidance and comfort. Before he is interrupted, Yorick contrasts thirty minutes of mediocre and self-referential pontification with "five words point-blank to the heart". As with the flap, here Sterne appears to suggest that only some kind of jolt enables us to develop new and better spiritual insights.

The 18th century saw many instances in which head and heart were described as distinct spheres of human sympathy and different agents of action. One reviewer described Sterne's printed sermons as preaching to the heart, and in keeping with both reason and scripture. The same critic understood Sterne's intention to be aimed at "mending the heart" and, by it, to impart moral virtues and improve society. Too often sermons would become a fashion parade of theological learning, adding very little to the lives of those obliged to listen. Clearly, Sterne believed in preaching that was more than mediocrity adorned with tinsel.

10. Saturday

Charity and Choices

Many issues relating to charity are as old as humanity. Not least decisions about *who* to help and *how* to help. In *Tristram Shandy*, the country parson - Yorick - has the expense of maintaining a good horse, and has one or two other horses besides. All well and good. However, as the nearest midwife to the village was seven miles away, for one reason or another, the parson received regular applications for the use of his good horse. As those who borrowed the beast did not necessarily use it well, the result was that the horse became "either clapped, or spavined, or greazed;- or was twitter-bone, or broken-winded, or something…".

Consequently, the cleric faced significant expense in the regular replacement of the animal. Over time he realised that the cost of maintaining this provision meant he was unable to offer "any other act of generosity in his parish". As it was, the horse was chiefly used to fetch the midwife. This led to thoughtful consideration about the charity which could not be given when so much was committed to one asset. The narrator in *Tristram Shandy* reflects that for Parson Yorick:

> It confined all his charity into one particular part of his parish; reserving nothing for the impotent,- nothing for the aged,- nothing for the many comfortless scenes he was hourly called forth to visit, where poverty, and sickness, and affliction dwelt together.

It has been the practice of clergy long after Sterne to provide funds for those in greatest need. In the autobiographical novel *Country*

Boy by Richard Hillyer, the local parson accompanied regular home visits with the dispensation of a shilling or two, where most needed. This was in the early 20th century. Today this kind of assistance is often more structured and accountable, but churches continue to provide help wherever possible and as fully as they can.

Sterne often identified with Parson Yorick, even publishing his sermons under the fictional name. It is easy to imagine Sterne at Stillington, or Sutton-on-the-Forest, finding it hard to say "no" to urgent requests but finding the cost of regularly replacing his horse would be a significant drain on his resources. It also left him in situations where he wanted to provide aid but found himself unable to do so - or not to the extent that he wished. There is evidence of Sterne covering costs for some of the poorest in his parishes, but there were inevitably limits to what could be done. Sterne came to develop a strong income through his writing, but he lacked an endowment or annuity that generated funds or acted as a reserve.

Parson Yorick decided to dispose of all but one of his horses. He rode around on this more humble steed to preserve funds for other acts of charity. He does not neglect the need that has brought him to this decision, purchasing the licence and other essentials required to set up a midwife locally. However, the narrator carps about how these actions may be interpreted by the parishioners; that it was all about the parson's pride to ride in style, and nothing to do with any act of pastoral care and generosity.

Of course, in this fictional narrative - however autobiographical - Sterne is uniquely placed to defend his conduct and refute his critics. Most of us are not in such a fortunate position. Living with the misconstrual of our intentions is an ever-present reality, and we cannot always explain why a particular course of action is deemed best. These issues for Jesus occur at a very different scale and consequence. A significant part of the Gospel story is that Jesus is misunderstood, time and again. When, on the cross, Jesus was taunted with the words "He saved others but he can't save himself!" two misunderstandings are implied. Firstly, that Jesus has the power necessary to extricate himself, but refuses to use it (is this a form of suicide?) or secondly, that he isn't the Son of God and, like us, has "no power of himself to help himself" - thus proving his self-deception.

For Sterne what mattered in charity was the purpose that generated the gift. With both benefits and injuries, "we consider no part of them so much as their intention". The intentions that are rooted in our actions become the yardstick by which the quality of a gift is understood.

Week Two

11. Monday

Humph!

Sterne's evident commitment to the Church of England is accompanied by a critical attitude towards other denominations. Jibes about Methodism and Roman Catholicism pepper much of his writing, whether in sermons or fiction. In *Tristram Shandy* this is not without a good sprinkling of humour. The character of the man-midwife, Dr Slop, is said to be based on the life of the York physician, Dr John Burton. Burton was a pioneer in obstetrics at a time when the scientific understanding of birth - and the practical measures to make it safer - were developing at pace. Burton was also identified as a Catholic sympathiser and Jacobite, which brought him into conflict with Laurence Sterne's influential uncle, the Precentor of York Minster, Jacques Sterne.

In *Tristram Shandy,* an episode is described in which a sermon is read in the parlour of Shandy Hall, in the presence of Dr Slop and the Shandy brothers. (Sermons by notable preachers were often printed and might form the basis for an impromptu discussion). The Shandy brothers are figures who identify with the doctrine and established position of the Church of England. There is an entertaining interaction between the characters in which Toby Shandy, in genuine ignorance, asks how many sacraments there are in the Catholic Church. He is surprised by Dr Slop's answer that there are seven:

> Humph!—said my uncle Toby; tho' not accented as a note of acquiescence,—but as an interjection of that particular species of surprize, when a man in looking into a drawer, finds more of a thing than he expected.——Humph! replied my uncle Toby. Dr. Slop, who had an ear, understood my uncle Toby as well as if he had wrote a whole volume against the seven sacraments.

Sterne is a master of suggestion when it comes to the non-verbal forms of communication and how much might be freighted in a single sound: Humph! The domesticity of his analogy about Toby Shandy's expostulation marries a matter of significant doctrinal weight with an everyday rummage through a drawer. It indicates that, in Dr Slop's answer, Toby Shandy has found rather more sacramental rites than he thinks entirely necessary. There is a hint here of "practical divinity", the view that theology is not a task contained within the university, but the work of developing the understanding of the faithful and the practices of belief in daily life. In effect, in this encounter, Toby Shandy has found more means of religion than he feels are strictly required.

There are dangers in attributing too much to so little, but it is true that we often underestimate our impulsive interpretation of body language and exclamations. Sterne reminds us repeatedly in his writing that communication is embedded in many non-verbal perceptions and meaning strays far beyond the page. Hearers and readers have their own work to do, and this cannot be controlled completely by either the speaker, or an author.

I believe that Sterne was alert to the assumptions of our gaze and the familiarity of the world we inhabit. On visiting the Cathédrale de Saint-Pierre in Geneva I was struck by the different arrangement of furniture and the pride of place given to a small chair at the foot of the pulpit. This was sat in by John Calvin as he prepared to preach the Gospel according to his convictions, and further the cause of the Church's reformation. Throughout the building, it was clear that the ornamentation of the space had been stripped away and the absences were palpable. However, when I look at York Minster it appears complete and appropriate to its purpose. It's how I expect a Gothic Anglican cathedral to be. In actuality, the whole building is littered - inside and out - with the empty plinths where statues of saints once stood. Someone else would see these in an instant, but to me, they simply appear as a natural part of the fabric. If I was shown a computer-generated image of how the church would have looked in the 15th century, many elements of the building would be instantly striking.

Our inner "humphs" should alert us to the familiarities and prejudices we carry within, and how these filter so much of what we see and understand. We might not be able to avoid this, but we can be aware of it.

12. Tuesday

Joy is Not Methodical

> But when he was yet a great way off, his father saw him, and had compassion, and ran, and fell on his neck, and kissed him.

It has been argued that - beyond an odd opening line - humour is absent from Sterne's sermons. I beg to differ. In his text on "The Prodigal Son" he makes the passing observation that "joy is not methodical". In an era of Methodism's meteoric rise, and in a city where John Wesley preached repeatedly, Sterne's statement is a witty hit. The developing Methodist congregations, as yet contained within the fold of the Church of England, were known for their religious enthusiasm and a methodical commitment to religion. Sterne's riposte to this system of belief was no doubt unfair to the incipient Methodist Church, and his intention may have been to disseminate a witty retort for people to use in the sectarian squabbles of everyday conversation.

Sterne was a latitudinarian. Like many Anglicans in the Georgian period, he steered a line between Deism on the one hand, and religious enthusiasm on the other. During this era, "enthusiasm" was not a joyful exuberance, but a pious intensity seen as the antithesis of reason. Yet for Sterne, reason was insufficient in itself to express the experiences of a humane life. It is therefore a spontaneous joy, rather than enthusiasm, that is a fitting expression of our response to God. This was achieved through a belief that something of God is in each of us and we have the room to manoeuvre our spiritual destiny with the aid of reason.

In a parable as potent in feeling as "The Prodigal Son", Sterne cannot see how measured responses or methodical approaches would apply. The joy of the father is beyond words and reflects a joy that cannot be contained. He runs, embraces and kisses his child.

Many forms of the eucharistic prayer, central to services of holy communion, commence with the words: "It is our duty and our joy". If the human response to God was all duty it would become a very dry and miserable experience. Yes, we may need duty to carry us at those times in our lives when joy is distant, and the discipline of prayer is sustained by an obligation borne of our personal commitment. If, on the other hand, we perceive life to be a tale of unremitting joy, then it is doubtful that we are truly paying attention to what is going on. The key in the prayer is the word "and", yoking duty and joy together as the necessary components of a faith that is open and alive to delight, while retaining a spirit of discipline that sustains faith when joy seems a distant memory. The proportionate role of the two will shift, as we journey through life, but duty and joy belong together.

While Sterne expressed many sweeping and stereotypical views on Judaism, Roman Catholicism, and Methodism (he described Quakers as "harmless") there is evidence that his attitudes were amenable to growth and development. This took place, it would appear, through experience. In *A Sentimental Journey*, at Calais, Sterne portrays Parson Yorick encountering a Catholic monk who is begging for donations for the poor. Yorick is rude to the monk and gives nothing. When he has parted from the monk, Yorick realises that he has been ungracious and concludes that: "I have behaved very ill". Subsequently, the monk encounters Yorick again and offers him a pinch of snuff. Yorick, both convinced of his prior fault and perhaps now, impressing a young woman, offers his own snuff box, contents and all, as a gift to the monk because the parson had "used you unkindly". In response, the monk refutes that any offence was given and begs to swap snuff boxes. It is a touching moment in the story and Yorick (and Sterne?) reflects:

> I guard this box, as I would the instrumental parts of my religion, to help my mind on to something better; in truth, I seldom go abroad without it; and oft and many a time have I called up by it the courteous spirit of its owner to regulate my own, in the justlings of the world.

13. Wednesday

A Gift of Consequence

The "widow's mite" has long been a phrase that captures with economy the idea that modest donations may represent great acts of charity. It sets in context the realities of personal wealth and generosity, placing the cost to the giver as the primary measure of the gift. Increased giving has long been a feature of Lenten observance and Sterne reflects in his writing and preaching on the nature of what might be regarded as a genuine gift.

When I was a curate, the vicar and I visited care homes in the parish every fortnight. Dressed in our ecclesiastical finery of cassock and surplice we did our best to recreate a sense of church in a sitting room where chairs around the walls were jammed together, armrest to armrest. As part of this ritual, the vicar always insisted that after the service I took around the room a purse for a collection. At the time I thought this seemed a rather heartless act for our community's senior citizens, but I soon realised that for some residents it enabled them to feel that they amounted to more than simply being the recipients of care. They were contributing to something.

One woman in particular made a great impression on me. Whenever she received Communion in the service she responded with the startled words of St Thomas: "my Lord and my God". When the collecting purse came to her a five-pound note was pushed in. At the time, in the context of the level of state pension, this was a significant sum.

In *A Sentimental Journey* Sterne describes an encounter between Parson Yorick and a group of beggars as the fictional vicar travelled across France. In preparing to depart, Yorick encountered several of these poor souls gathered by his carriage. The atmosphere of pathos in this encounter is created by the observation that one figure "put something under his arm, which had once been a hat". This same individual then takes out a box of snuff and offers it to those present, including Yorick. Sterne describes it as "a gift of consequence" which initially Yorick "modestly declined". Yet the generosity of the man so moves Yorick that he places a couple of coins in the snuff box while, simultaneously, taking a small pinch of the snuff. As Sterne puts it, taking the snuff had the effect of enhancing the value of the coins. The gift was charity, but as to the acceptance of the snuff: it "'twas doing him an honour".

In common with many of us who are importuned for donations, whether on the street or elsewhere, Yorick protests that the money he had available to donate was all spent. In the same moment that this realisation dawns, an inner voice questions his duplicity:

> Good God! Said I - and I have not one single sous left to give him - But you have a thousand! cried all the powers of nature, stirring within me - so I gave him - no matter what - I am ashamed to say *how much*, now - and was ashamed to think, how little, then.

It is a commonplace of faith that charity is more than the discarding of our excess. There is a sense in these words from *A Sentimental Journey* that the traveller has factored in the cost of various incidental expenses, such as tips and donations to the poor. The encounter with the snuff-sharer unsettles the equilibrium of Parson Yorick. His inner protest that he has dispensed all that was available is confronted suddenly by the conviction that in reality, he has much, much more that he could offer. The self-deceptions with which we all live, and find ample excuse to tolerate, are laid bare in Yorick's encounter.

Sterne has no easy answer to the vast injustices he sees in society. In the case of slavery, he argues for abolition on the basis of our common humanity. In a charity sermon in aid of education he refers to some countries where education was funded by the state as "a publick concern". Attenuating his message to his audience, Sterne makes the case for free universal education because of the "many ill consequences which attend the want of it". In other words, it is "cheaper and better" to instil learning and values rather than pay the long-term price of rebellion.

For most people, a pinch of snuff would not be regarded as a gift of consequence. In the situation Sterne narrates, the value of the gift grows in proportion to the humility of the donor; the relationship the gift creates, however fleeting; and the honour conveyed by its acceptance. Sterne believes it is by looking away from, rather than encountering, the distress of the world that people stifle their compassion and restrain their impetus to act. His challenge is to "go into the dwellings of the unfortunate, into some mournful cottage, where poverty and affliction reign together".

14. Thursday

Wiser and Better

The rising influence of Puritanism in the 17th century generated an interest in "practical divinity". If religion in earlier centuries had appeared at times to create a separate and self-serving character, the reaction it provoked focused on the practical difference that a religious life might achieve. Something of this had been evident in the English reformations of the 16th century. When former religious foundations were recreated as hospitals, notably those in London, the chaplains were tasked both with practical matters (e.g. the supply of food) as well as the moral improvement of residents. One chaplain even became immersed in the medical work of the hospital, petitioning the governing body for extra pay due to his role in setting bones.

As we have seen, practical divinity continued to be a significant strand of church life in the time of Sterne. His sermon on "Pharisee and the publican in the temple" (Luke 18) castigates religious practices that focus on a mechanistic sense of obligation. The Pharisee's sense of "triumph and self-sufficiency'" should be seen as a warning of spiritual pride. In the attitude of the publican, by comparison, Sterne finds no plea of individual merit; comparison with others; or justification before God. As Sterne observed, "the best of us fall seven times a day" and pretending otherwise does nothing to further our spiritual development.

The critics of Sterne were concerned that candour about sin and personal failure might sometimes be a facade for the enjoyment of his shortcomings. Certainly, his characters (perhaps especially those with whom he identified) demonstrate an ease with behaviour that would undoubtedly attract censure. In Paris, Parson Yorick, feeling the pulse of an attractive shop assistant, is aware that doing this openly might attract moralising comments. However, as he says in *A Sentimental Journey*, "when my views are direct... I care not if all the world saw me feel it". This suggests, along with many other instances, that Sterne had a great capacity to be lost in the moment and go where his feelings directed. Only a few pages before this comment, on leaving his hotel, Parson Yorick's thoughts are described as follows:

> I walked forth without any determination where to go - I shall consider of that, said I, as I walk along.

For some this mixture of spontaneity and religious commitment was simply incompatible. Unless you study the guidebooks and plan, you might end up in the wrong part of town. Might a lack of planning be construed as an unconscious strategy to allow yourself to wander into temptation? Perhaps Sterne's model for his approach is the Prodigal Son. There appears to have been little planning or caution in the younger son's setting out, and his sin and salvation only become clear through his experiences once he had "walked forth".

No doubt we all approach Lent with differing levels of planning and determination. Whether to abstain from something, take up something, or even read a daily reflection - all observances carry the risk that the focus becomes the commitment rather than its consequence. Sterne encourages us not to exchange "the shadow for the substance". He argued that religion must be brought back "to that cool point of reason" where we are reminded that God is spirit and truth and that our best sacrifice is to offer God "a virtuous and upright mind". The practical end of religion is that we become better people, "better neighbours-better citizens-and better servants to God". Attending to the fruits of our faith, Sterne's theology is rooted in both practical wisdom and ethical sensibility. Religion should not teach us to harm or to hate.

The figure most frequently critiqued in his writing is the person who purports great sanctity while exhibiting behaviour that stands in direct opposition to their stated beliefs. Sterne's legacy suggests that he was alive and alert to disparities of behaviour and belief and, in a *Shandean* way, smiles upon the ridiculous figure cut by those who are mired in hypocrisy. By contrast, the Prodigal Son is loved because, when he greets the Father, his sins are neither disassembled nor cloaked.

15. Friday

A Different Object

The first article I ever published, concerning chaplaincy, took as its title some words spoken to me by the CEO of the hospital where I worked. In a meeting when we were discussing some aspect of hospital management, he suddenly commented in response to what I'd said: "it's like hearing the same things spoken about differently". In other words, while we were discussing an identical topic, the place from which I was speaking (with "place" including education, formation, vocation etc.) was different. I think he found it helpful. In any event, it was an early lesson for me that chaplains could bring a distinctive perspective, not a superior one, but one that spans both history and the diversity of places in which chaplains stand.

In *Tristram Shandy*, Sterne describes the "infinitude of oddities" which gave Walter Shandy a very unusual outlook on the world. It appeared that Walter's "road lay so very far on one side, from that wherein most men travelled". Consequently, it was very hard to predict "by which handle he would take a thing":

> that every object before him presented a face and section of itself to his eye, altogether different from the plan and elevation of it seen by the rest of mankind. - In other words, 'twas a different object...

The growing recognition of neurodiversity suggests that more people see a world that is altogether different from the "agreed" perception of the majority. We are not all on the same road and, in various ways across the breadth of human history, that difference has often been used as an excuse for punishment. In order to assure the majority of its normality and self-confidence, perceptual heresy has been identified quickly, and extinguished. I have been told that at one stage it was the usual practice to correct the "wrong" memories of people living with dementia and related conditions. That culture has changed, but we are still some distance away from fully recognising the illusory nature of a normative reality which the majority automatically assumes to be right and, consequently, enforces on those who diverge.

In Sterne's day modest wealth and good social standing might permit an individual to view the world somewhat eccentrically, without encountering excessive attempts to normalise it or punish it. Eccentricity, derived from a Greek word that has held its meaning with consistency over the centuries, means to be "out of centre". As with Sterne's description of Walter Shandy, this suggests travel down a different road and, consequently, the observation of an object from an unusual perspective. In turn, this may lead to a narrative account that sounds strange and discordant when heard by those looking at the same things from another place. Consequently, eccentric observations can be both richly informative and dangerously different.

Perhaps the degree of tolerance or acceptance of unique perspectives is highly dependent upon the independence and space afforded by wealth and social standing. When those factors are absent, divergence from accepted norms becomes far more problematic. In the final weeks of the life of Jesus, there is ample evidence that far too many important norms were being transgressed. Standing before Pontius Pilate, the refusal of Jesus to bend or shape himself around the patterns of expected behaviour and convention would lead to great sacrifice. Many of those who remain wedded to the integrity of their perspective know something of the agony in the garden. Who wouldn't want this cup to pass by? Conformity is a strong and beguiling temptation.

16. Saturday

All of a Piece

> She had heard that all was of a piece there, and that he was thoroughly consistent.

In telling the tale of the Shunammite woman and Elisha from 2 Kings 4, Sterne focuses on the offer the prophet made to use his influence to improve her lot. Having thoughtfully offered to build a new room in the house as a bolthole for Elisha when journeying in the region, Elisha offers to speak in the Shunammite woman's favour to the King or a senior official. The woman declines the proposal in a manner which is emphatic and conclusive: "I dwell among my own people".

In Sterne's reading of this story, the emphasis falls on what he calls "an instance of unaffected moderation and self-denial". The woman who offered Elisha hospitality is described as wealthy, and perhaps she understood the dangers of wealth when it is always seeking more, or ambition that can increase the risks of peer envy and court intrigue. Her response is not meek but wise. She is content amongst her own people and is happy to leave it at that.

When Sterne preached on the Shunamite woman he lauded the consistency of Elisha's conduct. This was what impressed the Shunamite woman about the prophet. We are not all of a piece when it comes to public statements and things said or done in private. Many politicians have discovered this to their cost. All too often we condemn in others behaviour we exhibit ourselves and seem momentarily insensible of the incongruity. When it comes to perceived sanctity and holiness, which Elisha exhibits, Sterne comments:

As such outward appearances may, and often have been counterfeited, so that the actions of a man are certainly the only interpreters to be relied on, whether such colours are true or false.

In any given age, conventions and accepted behaviours may differ from our own and, indeed, across society. There is a strong possibility that Sterne was unfaithful to his wife. There may have been ill-advised adventures in York, and later a close and romantic relationship with Eliza, many years his junior. As the presiding judge of ecclesiastical courts, he pronounced the punishments for those guilty of fornication. The risk of both a fine and public confession which went with this judgement (for the poor) was not a risk to gentlemen as there were exemptions for the upper class. Such a differentiation is hardly a surprise.

The theme of mercy and poor relief which is part of the narrative of Elisha and the Shunammite woman may have found echoes in Sterne's conduct.

She considered that charity and compassion was so leading a virtue and had such an influence upon every other part of a man's character, as to be sufficient proof by itself of the inward disposition and goodness of the heart, but that so engaging an instance of it as this, exercised in so kind and seasonable a manner, was a demonstration of his, - and that he was in truth what outward circumstance bespoke, a holy man of God.

Perhaps for Sterne "charity and compassion", as the chief virtues, spoke on behalf of those other behaviours which might tell another story about character. Yet for the Shunammite woman, if we take Sterne's perspective from the sermon, the proof of virtue lay in the consistency of conduct. The prophet's words and deeds were good, and so was his life. He was holy.

Sterne knew all too well that he did not always practise what he preached. He danced on the edge of many boundaries, not least life and death. As an undergraduate, he had woken one day to find his sheets covered in blood. Death was not some far-off event, but a figure that stalked him his entire adult life. More so than many of us today, Sterne knew that the end could come very quickly - at any time. Sterne described his intention in writing *A Sentimental Journey* as being "to teach us to love the world and our fellow creatures better than we do". It was an effort he made all his life, despite the setbacks and failures which befell him - or were of his own making.

Week Three

17. Monday

Winked into Suspicion

In the introduction to the Church of England's official form of worship, the *Book of Common Prayer*, there is a section entitled: "Of Ceremonies, Why some be abolished, and some retained". As this prayer book was written to be a primary instrument of the English Reformation, the text strives to explain why some rituals had been kept while others were discarded. The opening sentence suggests that, while some ceremonies began with good intent, these gradually became more superstitious than religious. Such that:

> because they were winked at in the beginning, they grew daily to more and more abuses.

This statement implies that past leaders of the church were not always responsible for initiating or promoting certain practices or rituals; but rather that they had tolerated such developments. This kind of feigned neutrality is a common characteristic of individual and organisational behaviour which warrants challenge. Contrary to appearances, the winkers are not innocent observers, but active participants.

I have always thought that the Church lacks a developed theology of winking. In my own ministerial experience, I have encountered people highly skilled in the use of hint and wink. Without evidence of any substantial reason, a nose has been taped or a facial expression pulled, to convey doubt or an implied uncertainty. I have no doubt that much of the disastrous history (and contemporary reality) of physical and sexual abuse lies in a culture of tacit behaviour. On at least one occasion I have written to a bishop about the perils of "hint and wink" when it was used to damage and undermine.

Alexander Pope's skilful assessment of Joseph Addison captures some of the characteristics of this damaging conduct:

Damn with faint praise, assent with civil leer,
And without sneering teach the rest to sneer.

There is something corrosive about this kind of behaviour, which manages to disseminate damage while appearing to be distant from the course of what follows. Sterne addresses this in a sermon entitled "Evil Speaking" inspired by the Letter of James, Chapter 1 Verse 26. In common with several of Sterne's sermons, this reference focuses on the self-deception of those who purport to be religious but who are unable to bridle their tongues. He describes the harm done to reputations by "distant hints, - nodded away, and cruelly winked into suspicion". Sterne knew from personal experience what he was talking about and had observed its consequences in the lives of others. Perhaps it was his growing understanding of this that contributed to the break with his uncle and one-time patron, Jaques Sterne, Precentor of York Minster. Jacques had recruited the young Sterne to be an anonymous writer of political journalism for the York press, but the relationship ended acrimoniously.

As the 20th century made so clear, the path to outrageous crimes relies on the careful grooming of a population. The steps to Guernica, the first instance of saturation bombing of civilians by air in Europe - immortalised by Picasso's famous painting - grew out of a regime in which the control of perception was a strategic priority. This, and many other acts of evil, are as much the product of people unwilling to act or speak, as they are of those who sign the orders. Mary Fulbrook has described this as the creation of what she terms the "bystander society".

The use of concealed means to manipulate people into complying with injustice has a long history. As the Psalmist says, "Sin whispers to the wicked, deep within their hearts" (Psalm 36). The need to weigh language and intention carefully, while attending to the possibility that we are failing to recognise fully the implications of our own conduct, is a necessary part of an appropriate humility. Arguably, for many of us, the *obvious* wrongs are not difficult to identify or to resist. The truly pernicious failings of humanity lie in that more difficult terrain of what Shakespeare termed the "honest trifles" that come to betray us "in deepest consequence". The seemingly generous gift that becomes an imparted obligation; and the half-truths that misdirect us from seeing the principal issue in a situation. By promoting awareness of such strategies, Sterne sensitises his readers to the hints or winks that damage reputations while simultaneously failing to deliver the evidence to substantiate what is implied.

18. Tuesday

Secret and Unseen

Taking his inspiration from Ecclesiastes 9:11 Sterne preached on the contrasting experiences of human endeavours. That in some cases, and despite all obstacles, one person appears to succeed, while at the same time, possessing every advantage and assistance, another person flounders while seeking to achieve their aims. I recall a faithful vicar many years ago reflecting that the people who everyone assumed would one day become bishops, didn't, while the most unlikely people did. Life is full of curious *snickleways* that facilitate the advancement of some while confounding the expectations of others.

Since the days of Sterne, we understand more fully that these passageways to preferment are neither arbitrary nor natural. A culture that appoints people who are different from the appointers is one that recognises and rejects the tempting appeal of "people like us". Often checks and balances are needed in order to foster a greater diversity of qualified candidates. It is possible that Sterne's sermon draws on some personal experiences. While very well-connected to senior figures in the Establishment, any ambition of greater advancement in the Church was scuppered by his first work - *A Political Romance*.

In 18th-century England, lotteries were very popular and funded a range of charitable and State objectives. For example, they paid for the building of the British Museum. It is therefore unsurprising, as Sterne reflects on the arbitrariness of life, that he should use the metaphor of a lottery. He wonders whether such a perception may incline some towards atheism. However, he concludes that reversals of human expectation are an argument *for* God's existence, rather than against it. Sterne felt that without God things would simply progress according to their nature. As he sees it, some other cause mingles itself in human affairs and resolves them according to God's - rather than human - will. Without God, a poor person would never become powerful, and a rich person would never be cast down.

For Sterne, the occasional and inexplicable change of fortune poses a question for which "You must call in the deity to untie this knot". Today other interpretations would be offered, but there is no denying a consistent thread across the scriptures that God is revealed in ways that confound human expectations. Not least in the Word made flesh and a way to salvation that involves crucifixion and failure. Sterne's God does not invade "liberty and free will" but influences our passions and desires which, sometimes, will cause the unexpected to happen.

In a humorous conversation about children who exceed expectations, a section in *Tristram Shandy* portrays a scene of risible male competitiveness. It is similar in tone to what many might know as "the Four Yorkshiremen Sketch". A conversation where competitive comparisons spiral down to a ludicrous level. The topic under discussion was children who were prodigies:

> Ferdinand de Cordouè was so wise at nine,—'twas thought the Devil was in him;—and at Venice gave such proofs of his knowledge and goodness, that the monks imagined he was Antichrist, or nothing.——Others were masters of fourteen languages at ten,—finished the course of their rhetoric, poetry, logic, and ethics, at eleven,—put forth their commentaries upon Servius and Martianus Capella at twelve,—and at thirteen received their degrees in philosophy, laws, and divinity:——But you forget the

great Lipsius, quoth Yorick, who composed a work the day he was born:——They should have wiped it up, said my uncle Toby, and said no more about it.

The flights of fantasy of the male speakers achieve the pinnacle of absurdity when Yorick suggests that Lipsius had written something on the day of his birth. Uncle Toby, in a manner characteristic of his wise and humble interventions in the book, hopes that this "work" was mopped up and forgotten. As is so often the case, men's fantasies and half-understood references push what might have begun as a sensible argument into the realm of absurdity. Toby's pithy comment grounds the discussion in some form of proportionate reality. Perhaps, when the fortunes of people do not go according to our expectations, for good or ill, we need to ask some basic and proportionate questions about what is going on.

19. Wednesday

Faint Civility

In his sermon entitled "Philanthropy Recommended" Sterne takes as his text the parable of the Good Samaritan. He describes the Samaritan as an "utter stranger" of the wounded man who fell amongst thieves. The story is told, Sterne contends, to rectify any "partial or pernicious" limit on the definition of who might be our neighbour. The emphasis of the answer Jesus offers falls on universal kindness and benevolence. In keeping with much of Sterne's thinking, common humanity is at the root of the Samaritan's generosity, who recognises that both he and the wounded man are "partakers of the same nature". In truth, "misfortunes are of no particular tribe or nation, but belong to us all". In providing care for someone of a different community and leaving the means of care even when he had gone away, the Samaritan acts without any implication of reward or other benefit. This generosity constitutes a true gift.

Elsewhere, by contrast with the story of the Good Samaritan, Sterne reflects on occasions when the offer of hospitality, or a gift, is experienced by the recipient as a "dry offer of faint civility". It is certainly true that we can experience a gift as a piece of social choreography: the bottle of wine that is brought as a gift when invited to dinner and, when the invitation is returned, a similar bottle passes back to the first host. How often have I heard during the visit to a family before a funeral "he or she would do anything for anyone", yet the English way is often a proud independence. People do not ask for help, hence, being willing to offer assistance when requested can sometimes ring hollow. Sterne says that at times generosity can be felt as a "cold and suspected offer". Greeks bearing gifts? It is wise to enquire about what is conveyed inside apparent largess and generosity - is it a favour which will one day be called in, or a gift to which nothing other than love is attached?

When Parson Woodforde, just a few years after Sterne, was busy being a parish priest in the wilds of Norfolk, he records in his diary a very touching gift left at his door. On 29th December 1786, he writes:

> Had another Tub of Gin and another of the best Cognac Brandy brought me this Evening about 9. We heard a thump at the front Door at this time, but did not know what it was, till I went out and found the 2 Tubs - but nobody there.

Readings used in the Church during Lent emphasise the desirability of making anonymous gifts (Matthew 6: 1-6). Jesus implies that we should be so discreet that we deceive even ourselves, so that our right hand does not know what the left is doing. This is a very strong teaching about the nature of true gifts, good works that are uncontaminated by any suggestion of reward or influence. Parson Woodford may well have wondered, but he could not know, from whom such generous gifts originated. Consequently, his ministry was not compromised. He does not need to suspect whether a supportive reference is wanted; or admission of a child to school; or a favourable view "bought" for an elderly relative's place in an almshouse. To quote Sterne, the anonymity removes any sense of "a debt of kindness unpaid".

We can all be bad at giving. Thomas à Kempis was right when he wrote in *The Imitation of Christ*, that a "wise lover regardeth not so much the gift of the lover as the love of the giver". Lent allows us to consider afresh the nature of giving, focusing more than anything else on the supreme gift of Christ to the world.

20. Thursday

Patronage

...full surely preferment was o' ripening...

In publishing *A Political Romance,* and seeing it withdrawn and burned at Archiepiscopal command, Sterne knew that his career prospects had also gone up in flames. He would not find himself, like his great-grandfather, living in Bishopthorpe Palace or even on the permanent staff of a cathedral such as York Minster. Sterne had committed the cardinal sin in church circles - he had told with wit and accuracy uncomfortable truths about the behaviour of senior clergy. While he might rely on the significant patronage of Lord Fauconberg, and the support of friends, Sterne had heard the doors to preferment close with a resounding thud.

Satire is a dangerous beast. Half a century earlier, Jonathan Swift had encountered a similar reaction following the publication of *A Tale of a Tub*. As with *A Political Romance*, Swift's book was his first significant literary work and cost him advancement in the Church. There are many echoes of Swift in Sterne's writing, including the use of digression and, in the case of *A Political Romance*, the allegorical role of coats. It is widely believed that Swift's use of satire denied him a bishopric and contributed to his exile from England to become Dean of St Patrick's Cathedral in Dublin.

The power of patronage can be very effective in shaping behaviour and silencing criticism. It follows that power not only corrupts those who wield it, but also does little good to those caught up in its web of influence. Recent years have shown how failures in safeguarding have arisen from a culture of deference and whimsical preferment. The risk of attributing decisions to the influence of unseen forces, such as the Holy Spirit, is that we do not take proper account of sin. For good or ill, much may hide under the label of mystery. There are silent instigators within human motivation and very often the Church has taken insufficient steps to recognise and mitigate these less attractive forces. Counterintuitively, the Church has failed to understand the limitations and compromises of fallen human nature.

In *Tristram Shandy*, the character of Parson Yorick is, at least in part, an autobiographical depiction of Sterne. In Chapter 12 of the first volume, there are references to the modest career attainments of the country parson. Yorick's friend, Eugenius, explains to the cleric the cost of too much wit and "unwary pleasantry", and that for every ten jokes he makes he acquires a hundred enemies. Revenge is the consequence of such wit. Eugenius warns Yorick:

> The fortunes of thy house shall totter,—thy character, which led the way to them, shall bleed on every side of it,—thy faith questioned,—thy works belied,—thy wit forgotten,—thy learning trampled on.

The main instrument of this revenge is identified as the prevention of preferment. In the unseen mechanisms of advancement, things were said or written that stopped Yorick's progress. The innocent parson is oblivious to this process and feels confident that he will soon see himself moved to a better position. However, as Eugenius recognises, "they had smote his root".

Preferment in the 18th century was an insidious process, known as the "patronage bargain". Quite simply, this meant that the gift of a position came with strings of obligation ensuring loyalty and support. This did not always endure, as we can see when Laurence fell out with his uncle, the Minster Precentor, Jacques Sterne. The Church of England still lives with the vestiges of this system, although the processes of appointment have greater transparency. It is impossible to say how much power and influence flows below the surface of these arrangements. Certainly, with regard to inclusion and diversity, the Church has responded to some extent following public and political criticism. Nevertheless, the pace of progress has been slow. The power of patronage is seldom renounced - all too often it must be prised out of someone's hands.

As Yorick approaches his death, Eugenius tries to rally the fading parson, saying that he hopes "that there is still enough left of thee to make a bishop". Alas, poor Yorick replies that his character has been so abused and knocked out of shape that even if mitres fell as thick as hail, none of them would fit. Patronage had abandoned him. Nevertheless, it's hard not to think of Sterne, with a twinkle in his eye, suggesting that even when one of the lower clergy is at death's door, and all appears to be lost, there is still sufficient material left to make a bishop.

21. Friday

Kissing Hands

In every age, there are mechanisms of progress which help or hinder careers. These processes are not of our choosing and may be interpreted as hoops through which we must pass, or not, as the case may be. We saw in yesterday's reflection that Sterne was able to portray in the humour of his novel the serious point that clergy could pin all their hopes on advancement and find that they come to nothing. Without the resources of inherited land or investments, Sterne was consigned to scrape by as best he could. There was little choice other than to manage the relationships that could ease his progress in the world although, as the falling out with his uncle suggests, there was a point beyond which Sterne could not, or would not, pass.

The final volume of *Tristram Shandy* begins with a dedication Sterne is penning for "A Great Man". In the literary world this was the route to enhance the support of a patron and, in the process, indicate the writer's allegiances. These influential figures brought not only money and pensions, but parishes that were in their gift. All of this could make a major difference to the life of a struggling artist or parson. In this dedication in Volume 9, Sterne is amending the dedication with which he began *Tristram Shandy*, noting that the former commoner and Prime Minister, William Pitt, had by this time been ennobled as Earl of Chatham.

Although Sterne was a participant and beneficiary in this system, it is clear that he saw its temptations and weaknesses. As part of the dedication Sterne reflects on the differences between imposed value and inherent worth:

> Honours, like impressions upon coin, may give an ideal and local value to a bit of base metal; but Gold and Silver will pass all the world over without any other recommendation than their own weight.

In amending the dedication to reflect Pitt's changed circumstances, Sterne shows a characteristic amount of cheek. His original, *a priori*, plan had been to dedicate the book to the commoner. Now he was making the dedication after the event, *a posteriori*, to the Viscount. When an honour has been conferred the final act of gift and reception is made in the kissing of hands - a custom that still exists for several offices in the British Establishment, including the moment someone is made Prime Minister. During the brief premiership of Liz Truss, she travelled to Balmoral to kiss the hands of Queen Elizabeth II in order to assume her office. In *Tristram Shandy* Sterne comments that "*a posteriori*, in Court-latin, signifies, the kissing of hands for preferment - or anything else - in order to get it".

The reader should understand that the term "kiss arse", meaning someone who behaves obsequiously, was in use in British English from the early 1700s. In the close proximity of Sterne's use of *a posteriori* (which I do not feel needs clarification) and the kissing of hands, "or anything else" to get a position, Sterne gives humorous expression to the kind of unfortunate behaviour which preferment often induces. At this point in the book, the focus of the text is directed to "the jealousy of their Reverences".

Preferment could silence people who relied upon it for their livelihood. Like an invisible force, the power of influence in appointments had unspoken consequences. Only slowly, with greater scrutiny, does this unseen hand of favour begin to emerge out of the mist. It might be argued that Jesus chose his disciples at will, but the similarity does not go far. These were not people recruited for material favour and advancement, but very often to endure cruelty, hardship and death. Jesus made no effort to court temporal religious power or climb through the ranks of priestly orders. On the contrary, Jesus called out base metal for what it was - no matter how much it was stamped with officialdom. In his interview with Pontius Pilate, the issue of authority is raised and questioned. When it is not inherent, as with God, power is always delegated. Across the gospels, Jesus suggests that it is among the poor and the oppressed, the foreigner and children, that the weight of true gold could be found.

22. Saturday

Uniqueness

Dear reader, by now you may have had your fill of Laurence Sterne, the 18th century and the sermons preached to the long dead. On the eve of Mothering Sunday, also known as "refreshment Sunday" coming, as it does, at the midpoint of Lent, perhaps it is time to lay words aside. As we shall, in a moment.

Perhaps *Tristram Shandy* was too hot for London - too controversial or innovative. Maybe there simply wasn't the appetite or capacity in the capital to take on this surprising project. In any event, it was not accepted for publication. Consequently, Sterne turned to a York printer, the recently widowed Anne Ward, whose premises were a short distance from the Minster. The author paid for the publication of the first two volumes and was rewarded with the immediate popularity of the title. This opened the way for subsequent publication in London. In volume three Sterne pressed forward his creativity, securing the inclusion of a marbled page amid every copy. As each page was hand-marbled (and therefore, unique) the costs of production must have been significant. The success of the first volumes no doubt empowered Sterne's ability to effect this inclusion.

Sterne described the marbled page as the "motley emblem of my work". Scholars have argued ever since about the significance of the emblem. Marbled pages were not unknown, but they were typically found in the presentational structure of a book, often employed as endpapers. Was Sterne intending to startle his readers - hinting that the end was coming sooner than they expected? Or was the page, like some other examples in the book, a sign that text always strays into the non-verbal parts of the reader's fluid imagination?

Perhaps it is a vivid statement of life's random events and the theme of digression that haunts Sterne's masterpiece. Another possibility is that the uniqueness of the page and, consequently, of every copy of the book, asserts that when text meets the reader it becomes a singular event.

If the intention of the marbled page was to imply individuality, Sterne does not make a direct link to the implication that the Bible itself may be read differently by each person. When the characters in *Tristram Shandy* read and discuss a sermon in the pantry, it is spoken aloud and debated. This provides an insight into life in the 18th century, when a sermon might well launch discussions over the Sunday dinner table, or during the working week. Individual understanding would meet critical responses and the testing of ideas in daily life. In the 18th century sermons were published - and bought - in abundance. A first edition might be awaited with keen anticipation. While each marbled page was unique, every page shared a common style. Their qualities and character were familial, even as they framed distinctive patterns.

In honour of Sterne's reverence for the unsaid and the unsayable; for his love of digression; and to make each copy of this book a reflection of the reader's uniqueness - I offer a marbled stencil. Respond to this as you wish, or leave it as it is, and I hope that something will flow beyond words and bring a moment of refreshment. In doing so, you will be making this copy of the book unique.

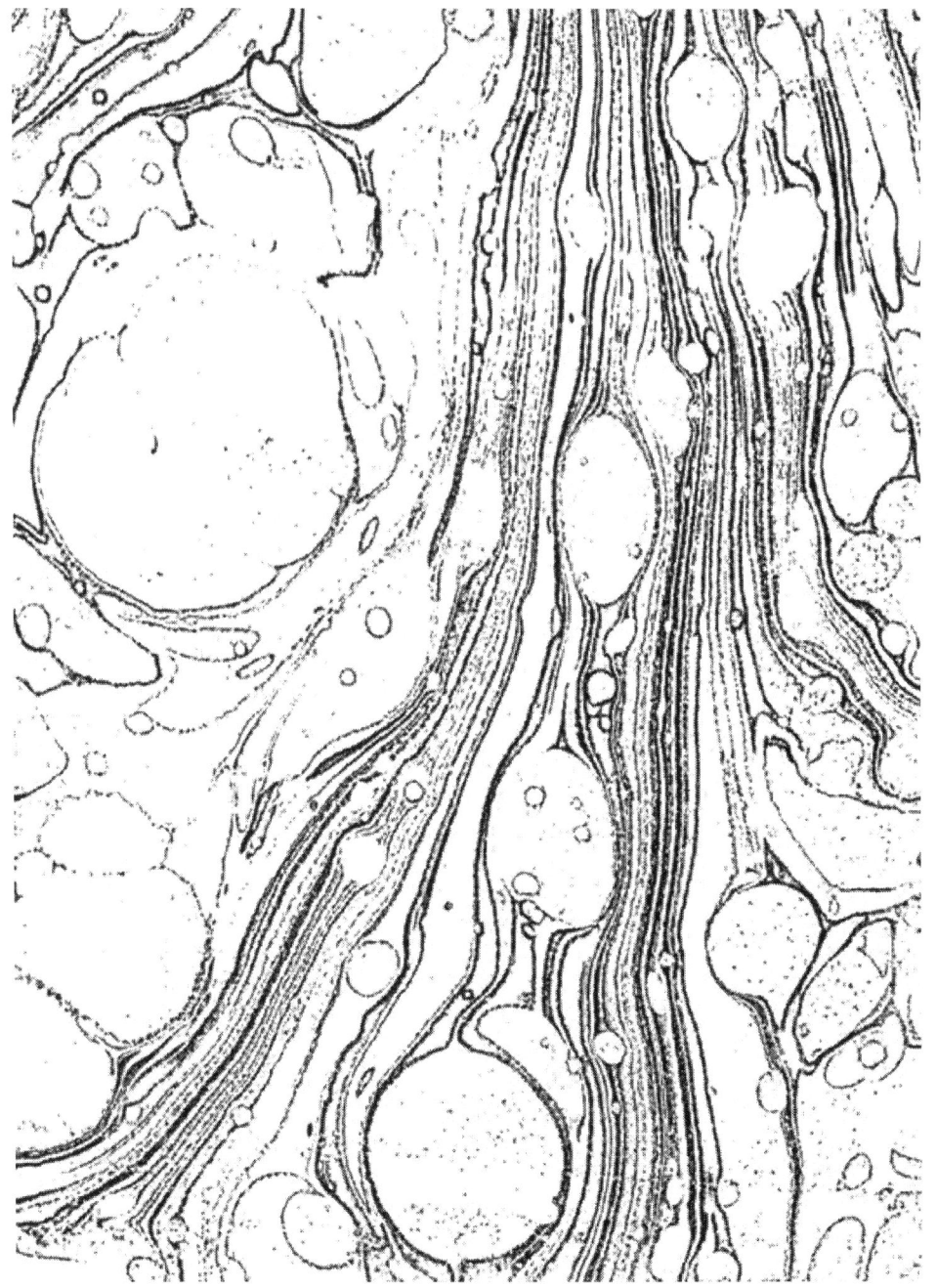

Week Four

23. Monday

Because they are not

Many times, I have knelt by the side of a cot, an incubator or a bed, and said words that rang hollow in a place of desolation. No words can bring meaningful comfort. The death of a child, from early in pregnancy to stillbirth at full-term, is one of the most awful events that anyone can experience. For chaplains it can be a very challenging situation, partly because the chaplain and family are probably meeting for the first time and a relationship of pastoral care must be established quickly with great sensitivity. The chaplain knows that nothing can lessen the sense of loss or the dawning realisation that an imagined future no longer exists. It is a harrowing experience for parents, families and hospital colleagues.

In a sermon Sterne preached just after Christmas, on Holy Innocents' Day, he took as his text Matthew 2:17-18. It is a text that refers to a voice heard in Rama, of lamentation and bitter tears: "Rachael weeping for her children, refused to be comforted, because they are not". Rachael, who had died during the birth of Benjamin, is portrayed in this prophecy as a matriarch lamenting her descendants as they pass by her tomb en route to exile in Babylon.

On one occasion, I attended a family as they awaited the death of a much-loved son. He was not a baby or a child, but a man in his mid-50s. In his childhood he had been caught up in a disaster at a public event, witnessing things no adult should ever see, let alone a child. The family told me that his memory of that disaster never left him, and that the seed of the events leading to his untimely death were very much part of his past. He was the latest victim of a tragedy but would never be accounted for in the number of deaths attributed to that fateful day.

In our pastoral conversation, his mother suddenly asked: "What about Gaza?" Here was someone with the knowledge of how disaster and suffering continue to exist in the lives of young people confronted by terrible events. Her question pressed ahead to wonder how those children now aged 5 or 6 will be in the year 2060. Tragedy has a powerful way of lingering long after the cameras and media attention have departed. Shelly Rambo writes cogently about the aftermath of Hurricane Katrina in the USA and the desire by so many people, once the storm had passed, to think everything was OK. Shelly quotes a pastor saying: "the 'after the storm' is always here".

The Sternes knew the experience of loss close to birth. In 1745, their daughter Lydia died within 24 hours of being born. This was probably just a few years before the sermon on Holy Innocents. As Sterne imagines the response of the mothers of the children Herod ordered to be slain, his choice of language might be viewed as 18th-century sentimentalism. However, there are grounds to believe that his focus on compassion is a strong component in crafting words for a congregation where many would have been touched by the experience of infant mortality:

> Every Bethlemitish mother involved in this calamity,
> beholding it with helpless sorrow - gave vent to it - each
> one, bewailing her children, and lamenting the
> hardness of their lot, with the anguish of a heart as
> incapable of consolation, as they were of redress.

As Sterne observes, such an event is "so circumstanced with horror, that no time, how friendly soever to the mournful - should ever be able to wear out the impressions". People who have lived through this kind of disaster know that the experience remains with them for life. It changes, but it is ever-present. As the son of a soldier, a pastor and a parent, Sterne knew first-hand the passion of loss and the duration of the damage wrought by violence and tragedy. While there is humour in his fond portrayal of Uncle Toby, the wound he received in battle is ever-present and the allusion to impotence implies a future possibility that has vanished.

Sterne's sermon concludes with a turn towards ambition, a danger he identifies across his writings, even while he knows its siren call himself. It is Herod's determination to preserve his power at all costs which gives rise to the calamity of Holy Innocents:

> Consider what havoc ambition has made - how often the same tragedy has been acted upon larger theatres - where not only the innocence of childhood - or the grey hairs of the aged, have found no protection - but whole countries without distinction have been put to the sword, or what is as cruel, have been driven forth to nakedness and famine to make way for new comers under the guidance of this passion.

Based on references in Sterne's correspondence, the sermon was most likely preached in December 1758. In a matter of a few months following this occasion, Sterne would publish both his satire directed at the ecclesiastical politics of York and, a little later, the first two volumes of *Tristram Shandy*. In all of this work, ambition flows as a ubiquitous preoccupation. Tragically, parents continue to weep for their children, their land, and their livelihoods, while no amount of destruction seems to slake the thirst of men's ambition. It is little wonder that Rachael weeps.

24. Tuesday

A Small Pipe

There is little allowance made in some sections of *Tristram Shandy* to the capabilities of the reader. Or, as some have suggested, the book was aimed at the well-educated in order to filter the readership and avoid a less refined audience sensationalising aspects of the story. For example, the advertisement placed in the local York newspaper for the book in late 1759 contained some text in Greek. Also, at one point in the novel, a genuine letter is reprinted, entirely in French, with no translation provided.

The letter appears in Chapter 20 of Volume 1 of *Tristram Shandy*. Immediately before the letter, the author makes a direct address to the reader. This address is about the danger of misreading a text and drawing false conclusions. Highlighting an example of imagined misunderstanding, Sterne hopes that both male and female readers will - by the example he cites - "be taught to think as well as read".

Tristram Shandy has a lot to do with both birth and impotence. The letter in French concerns the subject of emergency baptism. As a hospital chaplain, attending the delivery and neonatal units to conduct a blessing or Christening was a relatively frequent part of my ministry. Sometimes, the question arose in circumstances where the baby was not expected to be born alive. While on some occasions the family members present were content for a blessing to be said, there were times when the desire for baptism was overwhelming and desperate. I shall never forget the time I was called to see a woman who had been told that her baby had died in the womb, close to full term. She was about to undergo an induced delivery. "All I want", she said, "is for you to baptise this baby when it's born".

The view of the Catholic Church in Sterne's day was that at least some part of the baby must be visible for a baptism to take place. It is why in *Tristram Shandy* the man-midwife, Dr Slop, carries a "squirt" in his bag. This could be used to baptise a baby as soon as any part of it emerged into the world - when the risk of a stillbirth was anticipated. The letter in French is a Memorandum of the Doctors of the Sorbonne responding to the suggestion that technological advances meant that baptism could, in extremis, be achieved in utero through the use of a "small pipe" (or cannula) by which holy water would be administered without any problem for the mother.

> Le Chirurgien, qui consulte, prétend, par le moyen d'une petite canulle, de pouvoir baptiser immediatement l'enfant, sans faire aucun tort à la mere.

> The surgeon who raises the question asserts that by means of a little injection-pipe he can baptize the child directly, without doing any harm to the mother.

In this debate, Sterne is not oblivious to the dubious nature of a suggestion being made by male medics and theologians. No doubt these learned gentlemen sat comfortably as they debated the theoretical implications of a male doctor inserting a pipe into a woman in order to conduct a baptism. It would, of course, do her no harm.

In his imaginative response to this scholarly discussion, Sterne takes the argument a stage further and suggests that one way to avoid any doubt in the matter would be to baptise all of a man's sperm. (This reflects thinking at the time that there was a fixed stock of sperm containing "homunculi" - minuscule people ready to grow once implanted in the womb). Hence, Sterne concludes the chapter by suggesting that a little injection-pipe could be inserted into the man, between marriage and consummation, to ensure a "shorter and safer" way to baptism.

Simultaneously, this passage in *Tristram Shandy* hints at how emerging medical technology might affect sacramental practice, while lampooning male pontifications that determine what will, or won't, do any harm to women. In pushing the ideas further, Sterne discomforts his male readers - and certainly amuses his female audience - in suggesting that sticking a cannula into a penis would be altogether more effective. His final words in the chapter are: "sans faire aucun tort au père": without doing any harm to the father. The reader is left to ponder whether male theologians and medics would sit quite so comfortably at the thought of such a solution.

"Baptism of the homunculi" by Rob Oldfield (reflection 24)

25. Wednesday

Last Things (and First Things)

The last thing my father asked me to do for him, before he was admitted into hospital shortly before his death, was to wind up the mantelpiece clock.

He had always enjoyed clocks and watches. As an engineer, he liked to tinker with a timepiece and repair it if he could. There was a small drawer at home where various semi-dismantled watches were kept. In later life, this particular interest waned, although his general interest in clocks persisted. In the early stages of dementia, my mother developed a confusion about time. She was losing her eyesight, and this made it difficult for her to read the face of her watch. Then a determined idea grew in her that time had in some way become unreliable. In hindsight, I wonder if the annual practice of changing the clocks to Summer Time had sown the seed that, somehow, time had been corrupted.

In order to help my mother orientate herself and recognise the right time, my father decided to buy a clock with a sizeable face which would chime on the hour. I don't recall that it made any difference to my mother's sense of time, but my father was fond of the clock. With his wife now living in a care home, the clock kept him company in his small apartment. It did not keep perfect time and therefore, along with winding up the mechanism with a key, it was necessary to adjust the minute hand each day. As my father's mobility became slower and increasingly difficult, with prostate cancer spreading more widely, he asked me to perform this small task of correction and re-energise the spring. I now have the clock, whose time will far outlast my own time (so long as it is wound up).

For Sterne's character Tristram Shandy, winding up a clock was key to all his troubles. It was not a task at the end of his life, but at the beginning. So much at the beginning that it opens the novel and concerns Tristram's conception. Tristram's father was wont to unite a number of domestic duties on the first Sunday in the month. These included sex with Mrs Shandy, as well as winding up the large house clock. As it happened, in March 1718, the time of Tristram's conception, the first Sunday in the month was also the first Sunday of Lent. It may have been a "sacrament day", as some churches observed the regular celebration of Holy Communion on the first Sunday of the month. All in all, Mr Shandy was having a busy day when, in the midst of conceiving Tristram, his wife asked: "have you not forgot to wind up the clock?"

The interruption of Mr Shandy leads to an exclamation and, as Tristram would come to see it, the fatal blighting of his future prospects. As we have seen, it was Sterne's understanding (or satirical view) that tiny proto-people - *homunculi* - transferred from a man to a woman in the act of conception, were accompanied by the "animal spirits". The latter determined the vigour and natural strengths of the child. As the reminder to "wind up the clock" was an interruption at precisely the wrong moment, the animal spirits accompanying Tristram to his "place of reception" in Mrs Shandy underwent a disturbance with enduring consequences:

> my little Gentleman had got to his journey's end
> miserably spent;—his muscular strength and virility
> worn down to a thread;—his own animal spirits ruffled
> beyond description…

Moments in time have the capacity to alter the course of events far beyond the instant in which they occur. While Sterne's satirical portrayal of the homunculi, and the claims of science, may seem remote and of little concern, his overall preoccupation that life-chances are largely determined by the arbitrary circumstances of our birth, is not irrelevant.

Being "wound up" became a metaphor for Sterne concerning the energy of life and, in particular, the desire that leads to procreation. At the beginning of life, and at its end, we find ourselves in circumstances not of our choosing. We are unwound by events and must make of these the best we can. For Sterne, it is why moments of pleasure and delight are divinely given and should not be denied. Feeling ourselves to be truly alive and animated is a taste now of the life to come and the banquet that awaits us.

26. Thursday

The Duchess of Suffolk

Sterne uses many convoluted and entertaining discussions to dispel the murk of convention which, in any age, hangs over matters of consequence. Two of these issues are tied together very neatly in the fourth volume of *Tristram Shandy*.

Walter Shandy puts a lot of store on the idea that given names may come to have a profound effect on people's lives. He says that these names possess a kind of "magick bias", shaping the development of character and conduct. For this reason, at the birth of his son, Walter is concerned to ensure that the right name is given. As the women in the bedchamber recover from the exigencies of birth, Walter pontificates with his male friends in the parlour about the disaster which has befallen the newly-born Tristram. In a sudden crisis at birth, when baptism became an urgent consideration, a maid goes to the parlour to ask the father for the name he wishes the child to be given. Unfortunately, in rushing back to the bedchamber the maid miscarries the name. The child should have been called Trismegistus, but (understandably), the garbled message, and the curate's interpretation of it, settles on Tristram. For Walter, the name Tristram was the worst name that anyone could be given. This event, along with other circumstances of the birth, was believed to disadvantage all future prospects for the poor child.

A debate ensued amongst the men as to whether this error of naming could be rectified. Toby Shandy only interjects occasionally, and briefly, as this discussion evolves. When a statement is made concerning the validity of a baptism if it was misspoken in Latin,

Toby says simply: "Twas all in English". When abstruse arguments are made about the grammar of the baptismal words, Tony wonders "What do they signify?" When an appeal is made to the view of the Pope, Toby becomes exasperated: "But my brother's child... has nothing to do with the Pope".

There follows a remarkably unattractive discussion about whether a mother is a blood relative of her own children. This may seem to be an outlandish argument but, as we saw in an earlier reflection, many people at this time understood the mother's role during pregnancy as purely one of carriage and nurture, not co-creation. Consequently, in this view, the mother had no direct biological relationship to the child she bore. Unsurprisingly this argument had many significant and practical implications, not least in matters of inheritance.

When a discussion between a group of male church officers (during a meal following a bishop's visitation) began to reach its conclusion, it was observed that in a complex legal case regarding the Duchess of Suffolk, she was deemed not to be a blood relative of her child and, consequently, could not inherit the estate. At this moment Uncle Toby interjects:

And what said the duchess of Suffolk to it?

This simple enquiry brings the entire discussion to a halt. It was a male debate about money and inheritance, and it appeared to have occurred to nobody present that a notable figure had been cut out of the conversation and, indeed, the inheritance. Again and again, Uncle Toby asks obvious questions which, in a gentle but persistent way, identify key absences - or huge irrelevancies - in discussions that, in some respects are little more than the sparing of male egos, and in other respects revolve around matters of significant financial consequence.

In his letters, Sterne ridicules conventions that invest relationships between the sexes in commercial terms. Towards the end of his life, Sterne experienced significant financial exposure when one of his parsonages burned down. While there was no loss of life involved (a curate and his wife were living there) the cost of replacement fell to Sterne. Rebuilding a large, detached house was no small investment. While this matter remained unresolved Sterne received an application from a wealthy French gentleman who wished to marry his daughter. The applicant asked Sterne: "what fortune I would give her at present, and how much at my death". Sterne responded in the style of the request and began to offset the dowry according to her value. He begins by saying that the dowry would be £10,000. However, given that the gentleman was 62 and his daughter was not yet 18, he applied a discount of £5,000 to cover the difference. For her beauty and accomplishments (these are listed) Sterne feels that a balance has been reached and "finishes the account". It was Sterne's satirical expression of a flat refusal.

27. Friday

Consider Slavery

The local York newspaper of the 18th century was *The Courant*. Almost every front page of the paper in the mid-1700s featured two leading stories: war and news from the plantations. A war with the French, which England was beginning to win, and the economic exploitation of human misery: slavery. The remarkable and ground-breaking figure of Ignatius Sancho (the first black person in Britain to have his music compositions published; to vote; and to have his obituary published in a newspaper) picked up on a comment in a sermon by Sterne and wrote to him. The correspondence aimed to solicit Sterne's support for anti-slavery material in the later volumes of *Tristram Shandy*. However, as it transpired, Sterne had already written such a piece for inclusion in the next instalment of the book. The response Sterne sent to Sancho develops his rationale for supporting abolition, the appeal Sancho has made, and the female character Sterne created to articulate his point:

> on behalf of so many of her brethren and sisters, came to me—but why *her brethren?*—or yours, Sancho! any more than mine?

This is a striking expression of humanity and compassion, rooted in the dignity God gives to each person. In *Tristram Shandy* the dialogue centres on the question as to whether *all* people possess a soul, or only those in what was then perceived to be "civilisation". In considering slavery, the character Corporal Trim sees the lack of advocacy for a young black woman as the reason that people feel able to treat her badly: "because she has no one to stand up for her". In his reply to Sancho, Sterne asks the question, given the diversity of humanity, as to the point when "the ties of blood are to cease?"

More than 200 years before Sterne wrote these words there were debates in Europe concerning the relative status of human beings in different climatic regions. Some theologians had argued that there was a hierarchy of human dignity, which was weaker in the tropics. Others had asserted strongly that God could not have been so careless as to make people without souls. Sterne's comments echo the latter position, suggesting in his letter to Sancho that - in reality - there is no neat point at which to separate one group of human beings from another, based on physical difference. Our characteristics exist on a spectrum rather than as absolutes.

The fictional scenario in *Tristram Shandy* is a brief episode but, given the popularity of Sterne's writing at this point, it carried significant influence. In his correspondence with Ignatius, Sterne protests his willingness to act, even so far as to make a pilgrimage to Mecca, if it would ease the burden of all those who "have been so long bound in chains of darkness". As it was, including a brief episode in *Tristram Shandy* which centred on a young black woman was using Sterne's greatest power to influence change. He provides his characters with a discourse about the shifting nature of a nation's fortunes. Some may have power now, but will they in the future? When others are ascendent things may change. How power over others is used is part of this conversation. The brave "will not use it unkindly" and, by implication, bullies who use it unkindly are little more than cowards.

Sterne was not oblivious to the systems of ambition, privilege and power which operated in his world. The treatment of people enduring slavery, and the legal and social constraints that governed the place of women, were spun from the same yarn. When he wrote of the offer of marriage made to him, for his daughter's hand, Sterne portrays the calculation of cost, assets and benefit as little more than chattel slavery. To the extent that he can, Sterne is holding up to the light the reality of how power operated in Georgian England, and to whose benefit or disbenefit.

28. Saturday

Dance out the Answer

During a visit to France, Sterne suddenly realised that he didn't have a passport. Thankfully, through his reputation and connections, he was able to secure one without difficulty. This story forms the basis for a scene in *A Sentimental Journey*. In attempting to obtain a passport Parson Yorick finds an Anglophile member of the aristocracy (a Count) who is *un amoureux de la littérature anglaise*. In a room filled with books in English, Yorick attempts to explain himself to the Count. He picks up a copy of *Hamlet* and points to the name of his alter ego. This results in Yorick receiving a passport where his occupation is stated as "King's jester".

While the Count pops the edition of *Hamlet* into his pocket and leaves the room to sort out Yorick's passport, the parson surveys the remaining volumes of Shakespeare's plays. He decides to pick up a copy of *Much Ado About Nothing*. It is hard not to draw some inference from this choice. Sterne was a huge admirer of the Bard, and this selection may suggest a particular attachment to the story of Beatrice and Benedick. It is a play where the relationship of the sexes comes into particular (and humorous) focus. The refusal of Beatrice to marry implies an unusual nonconformity with the conventions of society. Her wit preserves her independence until, of course, the end. However, there is every indication that marriage will not diminish either her wit or her capacity to make judgements independent of male advice.

When it comes to the women in his life, Sterne offers a very complex picture. There are instances in his writing that demonstrate an acute awareness of the harm done by men deciding what is best for

Week Four

women. This relates not only to the birth of Tristram but also to the peculiar consequences of men's understanding of conception and the relationship of mothers to their children. However, in correspondence, as his life enters its final weeks, he writes to his daughter commending her to a friend from whom he hopes she will "learn to be an affectionate wife, a tender mother, and a sincere friend".

The ending of *Much Ado About Nothing* comes with a dance. While some commentators have suggested this represents harmony, it has also been argued that the sparks that fly between Beatrice and Benedick will now be contained, rather than extinguished. The dance is a mime of the relationship Beatrice and Benedick have portrayed throughout the play. They draw near and part; adjust their bodies to accommodate one another, or step away. They honour one another.

In the penultimate chapter of *A Sentimental Journey* entitled, "The Grace", Sterne describes an encounter with a farming family during Yorick's travels. The chaise had come to a halt and the good parson decides to seek assistance from what appeared to be a nearby French peasant's house. It turns out to be a farmhouse with about 20 acres of land complete with vines and a vegetable garden. Yorick is invited to join the meal being shared by an extensive family. After the meal, they all proceed outside where it was their custom to dance:

> I fancied I could distinguish an elevation of spirit different from that which is the cause or the effect of simple jollity. In a word, I thought I beheld Religion mixing in the dance:—but, as I had never seen her so engaged, I should have look'd upon it now as one of the illusions of an

115

imagination which is eternally misleading me, had not the old man, as soon as the dance ended, said, that this was their constant way; and that all his life long he had made it a rule, after supper was over, to call out his family to dance and rejoice; believing, he said, that a cheerful and contented mind was the best sort of thanks to heaven that an illiterate peasant could pay,—

Or a learned prelate either, said I.

The ending of *Much Ado About Nothing* does not offer perfection. Punishment is deferred until tomorrow, and many of the destructive behaviours are unresolved. Benedick calls for dancing before his marriage, and is contradicted by Leonato, who attempts to assert the normal order of events: "dancing afterwards". Benedick overrides this objection. Joy must be seized and celebrated when it is ready. It is little wonder that Sterne decides, out of all Shakespeare's works, that Parson Yorick should put into his hand *Much Ado*.

Week Five

29. Monday

The Last Inn

Death caught up with Laurence Sterne on the 18th of March 1768. It was the middle of Lent and Sterne knew that his life was ebbing. He was back in London, the city where his literary achievements meant that he enjoyed the best that society could offer. Sterne delighted in his fame but, in his final days, his thoughts turned to the care of his daughter. He wrote to a friend three days before his death begging that, if needed, she and her husband would act as parents to Lydia, his only surviving child. The concern of the dying for those who will continue to live is very understandable. Jesus, in his final hours on the cross, commends the care of his mother to John, the beloved disciple, and his care to her. They are to be as mother and son.

In care homes and similar settings, it is common practice to interview people about their last wishes. Often a conversation might be more difficult for the young carer than the older person, who has probably thought much more about their own mortality. There may be a discussion about who needs to be present at the time; or contacted; or what things might supply some comfort and consolation. Another question might be about *where* it would be preferred that the death takes place.

It is understandable that someone with a chronic health condition such as tuberculosis, who experienced frequent bouts of serious illness, would give thought to their final location on earth. For Sterne, one concern about dying at home was the thought of the attendant fuss. Equally, being in the centre of friends and family gathered around the bedside appeared to Sterne to be a scene of excruciating sorrow. In *Tristram Shandy*, he gives voice to this in the thoughts of the eponymous hero. Tristram thinks that the concerned attentions of his friends at such a time would "crucify my soul". These are strong words and may sound counterintuitive coming from someone for whom friendship mattered so much.

Tristram's preferred setting for what he calls "this great catastrophe", the final act of his life, would be a decent inn. Rather than being surrounded by sincere but sorrowful friends and family members, an inn would enable Tristram to receive the care he directs "with an undisturbed, but punctual attention". In some small way, this preference for paid care prefigures the best of the hospice movement. The setting is not clinical, but neither is it the person's home. The people providing care are compassionate and efficient, but they are not overborne with sorrow. Perhaps, unlike friends and family, they do not face the question of how life will continue following this death.

All these thoughts assail Tristram at the inn in Abbeville, as he travels from Calais to Paris. However, Tristram realises that not every inn could provide the kind of attention he desires, least of all the inn at Abbeville. So long as there was another inn standing, somewhere in the universe, the place of Tristram's death "should not be the inn at Abbeville".

While there is often a recorded preference in the medical notes of people's chosen place of death, these wishes do not always materialise. Circumstances alter the available options. Ideally, more attention is given to what might be possible and many medical teams that do all that can be done to meet the aspirations of someone nearing the end of life.

As Lent progresses there is a growing awareness that the death Jesus will undergo lies in Jerusalem. Many different lines of teaching, activity, prophecy and expectation converge on this sacred city. It is not the death Jesus would choose but neither is it the death he will evade. As he refuses to fit in with the expectations of the religious leaders or bend his knee to Rome, he is set on a course which will only end in one way. This moment will come as his closest friends flee the spectacle of his death, deny him, and hide behind locked doors.

It is good to enable people to make choices about what matters at the end of their life. There will be many times when all goes to plan - but often it won't. We envisage the future, but so often it turns out to be something different from our expectations.

30. Tuesday

A Creature of Few Days

In considering the disasters that befall Job, Sterne remarks that while such a succession of tragedies is rare "yet there are instances of some who have undergone as severe trials".

I was once asked to conduct a funeral "as briefly as possible". The family had experienced a significant number of bereavements and felt that they could no longer bear all the traditional elements of the service. It was simply too much and would recall all the services which they had already experienced.

As a hospital chaplain, there were rare instances when it was hard to comprehend the sequence of traumatic events which an individual or family had endured. Sometimes a close relative was in hospital themselves when someone died, and they could not attend the funeral. It was especially hard when a young person was one of the people being grieved. Mourning for a lost future is a poignant grief which can accompany a parent for a lifetime.

Sterne is roused to wonder in one of his sermons about the God who makes our burden heavier even as our strength grows less. I was often very moved to see frail people having to learn to walk again; or regain the independence to get out of bed; or even to re-learn how to speak. What would be a mountain to climb in the strength of youth is even harder as our resources of strength inevitably wane. I was once visiting a patient in a hospital bay when I overheard a physiotherapist speaking with a woman in another bed. "Come on Elsie, time to jump out of bed". Elsie replied, with dignity and irony, "I think my jumping days are over". She was 92.

In a sermon on Job, Sterne cites - but without attribution - a figure that half of the world's population died by the age of seventeen. Given child mortality in the 18th century this is a credible statistic. He wonders whether Job is correct that our short life is full of trouble. Here he considers war and the "barbarous devastations" where an entire nation is extinguished or is "driven out to nakedness and famine to make room for new comers". A reflection upon the book of Job seems, tragically, to be timeless.

Nor does wealth and privilege necessarily lead to a life free from sorrows. Sterne sees people of the highest rank "tore up with ambition, or soured with disappointments". Yet there is greater suffering among those "born to no inheritance but poverty and trouble".

Sterne's conclusion is that a sober assessment of the human condition should produce and sustain a spirit of humility. It should also incline people to spend at least a little time contemplating "that happier country, where afflictions cannot follow us, and where God will wipe away all tears from off our faces for ever and ever".

In pastoral ministry, the question of how we live in a context of suffering is often implied even when it isn't spoken. It remains one of the most frequently cited reasons why people struggle with faith, abandon faith, or remain steadfastly outside any community of faith. People are often humbled by the suffering they see and there can be both guilt and/or gratitude when the full force of another's experience strikes home.

Recently I came across a beautiful photograph on social media. It featured some undergraduate choir members from St John's College, Cambridge. They were sitting on a bench, robed but in casual postures, all looking at their phones. The service was yet to begin. In all respects, it was a picture of talented young adults, their lives stretching before them when the prospects for what is to come might be exciting and - as yet - largely undetermined. However, cropped into the frame of the picture, above them, is part of a funerary monument. At its base, still some way above their heads, was a skull. In a scene full of privilege, talent and promise the reminder of mortality held its peace. Over the centuries it had seen young people come and go, and there it remained, unchanged. We put great store by our lives and what they might mean: but the reality is that, in the scheme of the universe, we have but a few days. How we live sanely, faithfully and creatively with this truth is perhaps the greatest test of who we are.

31. Wednesday

Time Wastes

As with all parish clergy, as well as virtually everyone living in the 18th century, the experience of death and bereavement was an everyday reality. Sterne's father had died before his son had reached the age of 20. Laurence knew what it was to lose children in the trauma of their birth. Time spent in France was designed to improve his health but it did, consequently, bring him into company with other British exiles suffering from tuberculosis. On the continent in 1763 he befriended and supported George Oswald, a man in his early twenties, who was approaching the end of his life. At first, Sterne did not share with George the increasingly clear prognosis, however, when no doubt remained, he advised the young man.

On 2nd March 1763, Sterne wrote a letter sharing the sad news that Oswald had died. Oswald appears to have been a remarkably considerate person, asking Sterne to write a letter of thanks to a close friend and to his father. In the case of the latter, Sterne quotes the precise words which George wished him to convey: "That never did a Son leave a Father behind him with warmer feeling, of how much he owed you on this head, Than he did". Furthermore, George begged his father's pardon a thousand times for any indiscretions which had given him pain. There is more than a little of the Prodigal Son in these final wishes.

When Sterne told George about the hopelessness of his illness, he records that the young man said simply "God's will be done". In supporting George, Sterne was aided by a local Catholic priest of Irish descent. Sterne speaks highly of this priest although, when he dealt with different clergy while attempting to arrange a funeral for George, he had a very different experience. His efforts to secure a Christian burial were obstructed until, somehow, Sterne prevailed. In considering the character of George Oswald there is an additional piece of information which is both unusual and striking.

Oswald had been involved in a duel several years before and had begun to wonder whether an abdominal gunshot wound he received on that occasion might have led to the illness from which he would die. In order to ensure that no link existed, and thereby relieve his opponent of any sense of responsibility, George insisted that a postmortem should follow his death. Sterne was present for this the following day, which I can only imagine must have been a harrowing experience. It revealed that there was no link, and the gentleman concerned could be reassured that he had not caused the death of George.

Sterne knew about death and was keen to dodge its approach for as long as possible, He was mindful of the fleeting nature of our existence. I have been present on many occasions when someone's life has ended: with the newly born and the very old, and at every stage in between. Each death brings to an end a world of perception unique to the departing. Sterne, the country parson who had achieved such fame and recognition, knew that as the ink in his pen flowed, so did his remaining days. He was not a well man. While wealth may add to our years, through the advantages it can bring, the inevitability of death is a fact equal to all. Consequently, time becomes the most precious resource that we are given.

> Time wastes too fast: every letter I trace tells me with what rapidity Life follows my pen; the days and hours of it, more precious, my dear Jenny! than the rubies about thy neck, are flying over our heads like light clouds of a

windy day, never to return more ——everything presses on...

As Sterne writes in one of his letters, George Oswald died in his arms at 11 pm on 1st March. It was a sad end for someone less than half Sterne's age. While contemplating mortality Sterne recognised that in his writing lay some form of immortality and legacy. His mind, his skill and his imagination would continue to be experienced long after his corpse was interred. He can see no reason why his books may not "swim down the gutter of time", in a way similar to other notable works, and here I am, 250 years later, in conversation with this strange, complex, humane and compassionate figure.

32. Thursday

"You shall go home"

At various times Sterne suggested his identification with characters in his books. In *Tristram Shandy,* there is a very sympathetic portrayal of Toby Shandy, Tristram's ex-army uncle.

At an inn close to Shandy Hall, a seriously unwell army officer stops with his son while travelling to rejoin his unit. Word comes to the retired officer, Uncle Toby Shandy, that this man is unlikely to survive his illness. At first, all communication about the officer comes through Toby's servant, Corporal Trim. However, on the first morning of the officer's stay, Toby rises an hour before his usual time and proceeds to the inn. He visits the dying lieutenant, whose son is present, and Sterne describes the visit as follows:

> There was a frankness in my uncle Toby,—not the effect
> of familiarity,—but the cause of it,—which let you at once
> into his soul, and shewed you the goodness of his nature;
> to this, there was something in his looks, and voice,
> and manner, superadded, which eternally beckoned to the
> unfortunate to come and take shelter under him.

Uncle Toby lacks guile. He is straightforward, compassionate and frank, drawing the less fortunate to his protection. People who encountered Toby in their need found in him the kind of patient care and concern which established quickly a meaningful rapport. None of this was about the words used but arose from non-verbal exchanges and an elusive "something" that Sterne is unable to name. There is a hint in all this to connect the *something* with the spiritual. Perhaps it is Toby's inherent virtue that finds expression in looks, voice and manner?

The only thing Toby says to the officer (Le Fever) is the declaration that the lieutenant "shall go home directly... to my house". Toby has determined to accommodate the officer and his son and care for their needs. A doctor will be called and Toby himself will "be your servant". In the context of Le Fever's dying, there is a suggestion in these words of an eternal home. As we have seen in Sterne's sermon on the Prodigal Son, returning home can be a powerful metaphor for the place where we are met with love, forgiveness and celebration.

The scene at the inn illustrates a heartfelt compassion for the plight of a boy whose father is dying. In the brief time that Uncle Toby is in the room, Le Fever approaches the end of life. Sitting together as the witnesses of this passing are Uncle Toby and the boy. At one point a look is exchanged between them which Sterne describes as a *ligament* - a fine but enduring connection wrought in the trauma of parting. The chapter ends as Sterne uses the layout of the text to convey something of the faltering actions that accompany the final moments of the officer's life. For the end itself, the author chooses to draw a veil over the last breath.

——the pulse fluttered——stopp'd——went on——
throbb'd——stopp'd again——moved——stopp'd——
shall I go on?——No.

Sometimes, as with the death of George Oswald (reflection 31), Sterne provides a brief reference to religious practices that accompany the hours before a life comes to an end. These are usually simple and heartfelt. At the same time, Sterne pays particular attention to the *presence* of people who accompany someone in their final hours. Uncle Toby in this case and, a year earlier, Sterne holding the body of young George Oswald at the moment of his death.

Religious words and services have significant meaning and long histories of use, adaptation and authority. To quote Philip Larkin, they can be the rituals that robe our compulsions as destinies. Yet they can also feel useless, overly wordy and cumbersome when you are sitting with the dying. What matters more, it seems to me, is the silent love that gives us the courage to be present, even in this moment that witnesses the dissolution of body and soul. In our attention we extend the most tenuous ligaments of love, for a life that ends, and to lives that will never be the same again.

33. Friday

The Easy Man

In *A Sentimental Journey*, Parson Yorick is intrigued by a beggar who only seeks alms from women. Sterne notes, further, that the man appears to be very effective in his requests. On overhearing this beggar's conversation with two women, Yorick apprehends that skilful flattery lies at the root of his success. Consequently, Yorick adopts a similar strategy amongst the elite of Paris. Perhaps Sterne is affirming the issues also identified in *Tristram Shandy*, that getting on in society requires a degree of obsequiousness. However, as Parson Yorick's efforts progress, he experiences increasing disquiet about the cost of this behaviour. He describes it as "a dishonest reckoning"; "the gain of a slave"; and "a most vile prostitution". At the conclusion of these thoughts, he asks for his horses to be made ready for a departure the next day.

Systems generally foster behaviour that mutes criticism and secures continuity. The rewards for conformity are significant and the cost of dissension can be severe. For understandable reasons, most people appear to tolerate these arrangements to avoid the risks which criticism can generate. In TS Eliot's play, *Murder in the Cathedral*, one tempter appeals to Thomas Beckett with the words: "the easy man lives to eat the best dinners". Fitting in with the culture, and conforming to expectations, may bring the best fare but, as Sterne saw clearly, the cost can be significant. Of course, in the most consequential ways, Sterne lived within this culture. He accepted and courted patronage. Yet throughout his writing, he demonstrates a realistic appreciation of how bidable behaviour diminishes someone's integrity and potential.

I recognise within myself the observation made by the mother of Coriolanus to her son: "you are too absolute". Feeling the manipulation of power to conform stirs an opposite reaction in my mind and subsequent choices. It is a disposition that draws me to the figure of the resolute Christ of Holy Week. Riding on the tide of Palm Sunday's triumphal entry into Jerusalem, Jesus achieved the height of his political value. With either the High Priest, Pilate or the people, this is currency to trade and privilege to accrue. Perhaps Jesus could tone down the radical nature of his message and become part of the Establishment? Spending his entire working life in industry, my father often commented on former trade union officials who suddenly switched roles to become managers. The rewards would be significant in making such a move - effectively selling to management inside knowledge of union thinking and tactics.

During Holy Week the threads of power slowly entwine the figure of Jesus. Adulation is manipulated into hatred; friendship turned into betrayal; the life of a provincial rabbi deemed expendable; and the might of Rome exerts its defining power. In the midst of it all is one person. Someone who refused, time and again, to choose the kind of life that would lead to an easy dinner.

Sterne knew all about good dinners - and he ate them. But, as time went on, and the prospect of his mortality began to overshadow him, these meals became less and less satisfying. Friends became more important than his vanishing prospects in the church, and perhaps he began to realise that his writing would far outlast the temporary honours of high office or the ecclesiastical bureaucracy which might once have seemed so appealing.

Jesus was not an easy person for the religious authorities or occupying Roman forces. He was altogether too unbending, too unwavering, too absolute. Who did he think he was? His clarity of purpose became a rock against which the rules and conventions of the world broke and divided. Death appeared to be the obvious solution to such inconvenient behaviour - a way to put an end to whatever it was that Jesus might become. Putting your problems in the darkness of a tomb can have its attraction. After all, nothing grows out of what is dead and buried: does it?

34. Saturday

Fine-spun Notions

Paul's claim (or pronouncement) in the letter to the Romans is one of the shortest texts taken by Sterne in his sermons: "For none of us liveth to himself". These are words which Sterne imagines must astonish a "narrow soul" more than any other statement in scripture. He suggests that there will be people who simply cannot conceive that anything external to themselves should have a greater claim on their actions and purposes. Before his hearers can protest their disinterest and heroism, Sterne argues that if we strip naked our motives, and search the depths of our hearts, there is probably more self-interest than we care to acknowledge.

In his sermon entitled "Inquiry after Happiness" Sterne ponders both the advice that is given for the pursuit of happiness and the elusiveness of the goal. He gives the example of an honorific title as something which, when awarded, makes the recipient happy. However, he sees the pleasure associated with this recognition as something "found to be seated merely in the imagination". There are echoes here of the scriptural phrase used in every service of choral evensong: "he hath scattered the proud in the imagination of their hearts". Pride dwells in the deceitful power of our self-perception. In the same sermon, Sterne reflects on the nature of our progress towards happiness:

> When he has got thus far - if he is a plain and sincere man, he will make no scruple to acknowledge truly, what alteration he has found in himself - if you ask him - he will tell you, that his imagination painted something before his eyes, the reality of which he had not attained to.

Sterne was writing in the age of alchemy, the time when magic and chemistry did not stand so far apart as they do today. Many people sought a shortcut to power and fortune and foundered in the enterprise: "All had ended in smoke". King Solomon, wise and powerful as he was, experienced vanity and vexation of spirit in his efforts to find happiness in human endeavours.

However, despite our self-deceptions, Sterne cannot accept the view that human beings are completely depraved or devoid of virtue. After all, we are made in God's image - and our likeness to "the greatest and best of beings" indicates that we are capable of virtuous and selfless conduct. It is when we practise our faith, and as it de-centres our self-absorption, that unlooked-for happiness begins to steal into our lives. As we nurture a growing awareness of the nature of God, the eternal being, we discover a relationship with the Divine which sits uneasily with modern sentiments. We discern our own incapacity to act, possess, or direct. The "fear of the Lord" is a response to understanding the reality of our existence and allows us to place our happiness in the one relationship which cannot be lost.

While it may be biblical it is not necessarily fashionable to write about the "fear of the Lord". Nevertheless, according to scripture, it is the beginning of wisdom. For Sterne, this appears to be, to a significant extent, the opposite of our illusions of control and self-reliance. The fear of the Lord in this sense is a recognition that God is awesomely different from the nature of our existence. Most of us live for less than a century, compared with a God who spans time and eternity. There is a famous photograph, taken from the NASA spacecraft Voyager 1, called the "Pale Blue Dot". It was taken in 1990 at a distance of 3.7 billion miles from the sun. The picture shows Earth as the tiniest of blue dots, caught in a shaft of dispersed sunlight. Our planet looks like a mote of dust floating in a sunbeam. If it appears that we might be intent on destroying this blue dot, by arms or by pollution, this picture reminds us that it will make absolutely no difference to the universe. No difference. Reflecting on the suffering of Job, Sterne writes:

> God, for wise reasons, has made our affairs in this world, almost as fickle and capricious as ourselves.-- Pain and pleasure, like light and darkness, succeed each other; and he that knows how to accommodate himself to their periodic returns, and can wisely extract the good from the evil, - knows how to live.

Week Six - Holy Week

35. Monday

Secular Relics

When, in the course of my chaplaincy, I visit someone in their room in a care home, I always pay particular attention to the items that are present. Very often the pictures and artefacts are the result of a careful distillation that has taken place during repeated down-sizings. Perhaps from a family home to a bungalow, and then to an apartment, and now a single room. What is present represents a process of careful - and possibly painful - selection. Sometimes these items betoken a world of significance that may seem remote and strange to contemporary thought. For example, one resident was proud of her framed certificate of confirmation which hung on the wall. It had taken place in Ripon Cathedral in the late 1930s and its record had travelled with her across more than 80 years.

Often the items in a room may be expressions of connection with places of particular meaning during someone's life. Occasionally, a painting might depict a church that no longer exists - or is no longer in use as a place of worship. Always, there are pictures of people. These usually combine the continuation of life in the faces of children and grandchildren and the enduring presence of people no longer alive but remembered every day by those who may recall them with a tinge of sorrow. As TS Eliot wrote:

> We die with the dying;
> See, they depart, and we go with them.
> We are born with the dead:
> See, they return, and bring us with them.

Eliot, T. S. (1943). *Little Gidding* (p. 216). London: Faber & Faber.

Very often both the people and places connected with the images are connections invested with love. A place of childhood that brought joy and growth; the rites of passage that represent both continuity and change; the people who remain part of our identity and whose love persists. When I went through my father's things after his death there was a small envelope addressed to him in my mother's hand. It contained a brief note expressing her sadness that a plan to meet would have to be changed. I suspect that it was the first letter she ever wrote to him, and he kept it for more than sixty years.

In the religious world, the artefacts that connect us to holy people, and through them to God, are called relics. While the things I've mentioned above may not fall into that category, they possess many of the qualities that link a material object with people, places and events of spiritual significance. This notion occurs within *Tristram Shandy* during the love story of Mrs Wadman and Uncle Toby. The latter, who relished the detail and history of military campaigns, had a sentry box built in the garden overlooking a landscaped diorama representing the siege of Namur. It is here that he is courted by Mrs Wadman. As Toby explains military operations by placing his hand upon one of the maps pinned up in the sentry box, Mrs Wadman also places her hand on the map and, in the course of events, their hands meet. After the death of Uncle Toby, Tristram finds this map, which bears the fingerprints of both Toby and Mrs Wadman, and he vows to keep the map as it is, "whilst I have power to preserve any thing".

> By all that is priestly! I value this precious relick, with its stigmata and pricks, more than all the relicks of the Romish church—

What Tristram has found is a relic of love and a reminiscence of a late, lamented and adored uncle. The determination to ensure its preservation, unaltered, is a reminder of the tokens that have the capability to connect us powerfully with the people we love but see no longer. It is little wonder, on the sad occasions when an older person experiences a burglary, that the sentimental value of lost items is emphasised far more than any intrinsic worth. We are material beings, as well as spiritual ones, and it is unsurprising that we invest feelings in these tokens of love. In such a light it is understandable that in medieval times the trade in relics connected with the death and passion of Jesus became so widespread. These were physical connections to eternal love.

36. Tuesday

Only the Brave

Tristram Shandy infuriated some readers, and there will be plenty of people who never get very far into the book. Sterne confounds expectations, even in these early years of the novel, and he resists the temptation to write a story that leads incrementally to a neat conclusion. Taking inspiration from *Don Quixote,* Sterne's book portrays life as a series of events, some of which immediately appear to be meaningful, while others seem to be meandering digressions. It is this unusual narrative style that continues to stimulate contemporary artists and authors. Arguably, great art has the ability to enable us to recognise within its fiction a correspondence to life that is both real and illuminating. Perhaps few of our experiences seem to contribute to some grand design, whereas much of day-to-day life feels instead like a digression unburdened by any sense of meaning or wider connection. In the cases of Don Quixote and Tristram Shandy, any imagined noble enterprise becomes an increasingly doubtful facade beneath which everyday misunderstandings and disappointments teem.

In her Nobel Prize acceptance speech, the author Doris Lessing spoke powerfully about the role of creative stories in our salvation:

> Let us suppose our world is ravaged by war, by the horrors that we all of us easily imagine. Let us suppose floods wash through our cities, the seas rise. But the storyteller will be there, for it is our imaginations which shape us, keep us, create us – for good and for ill. It is our stories that will recreate us, when we are torn, hurt, even destroyed.

Of course, we do not need to imagine. Increasingly we see and experience the damage that is being unleashed by climate change and the ongoing wars across the planet. We certainly need new and better stories - ones that enable us to both imagine and desire more than the sorry accounts of hatred, distrust and revenge. The example of the cross is an acceptance of violence to end violence; the refusal to enter humanity's spiral of escalating destruction. Despite the hideous distortions of Christ's sacrifice that have fuelled anti-semetism and other ideologies of hatred, the unresisting acceptance of this path offers Jesus to the world as an example of a different kind of choice, and the interruption of the pattern where violence is seen as the only answer to violence.

In his sermon considering the history of Joseph, Sterne spends a significant amount of time exploring the practice of revenge. Repeating a theme which occurs in several of his other homilies, there is a comment that human fortunes can reverse and that we may "all be in another's power by turns and stand in need... of compassion". It is a cautionary note he also strikes in regard to human conquest and the operation of slavery. The consequences of responding in kind mean that "our revenges return upon our own heads". In this much, the behaviour of Joseph in forgiving his brothers breaks a cycle that may otherwise have continued unabated. For Sterne "only the brave know how to forgive", and it requires "the most refined and generous pitch of nature". The capacity to stay the hand of vengeance belongs to "a strength and greatness of soul".

The Bible is not short on references to a God who can become impatient, angry and destructive. The story of Noah, with its mass extinction of human beings, is perhaps one of the most extreme examples of this portrayal - albeit there are many others. Sterne, turning to the New Testament, quotes the teaching of Jesus about forgiveness, interpreting the saying "seventy times seven" as meaning a limitless capacity to forgive. He recognises that God alone can know how much human "practice keeps pace with the theory". We might talk about the need for peace and reconciliation but what are our actions?

At times we may be surprised by the absence of anger and revenge on the part of people who have suffered or been otherwise disadvantaged. In some cases, there may be a very Christ-like recognition that the perpetrators are caught up in a culture that is so endemic as to be virtually invisible. "Then said Jesus, Father, forgive them; for they know not what they do". Perhaps, as with the cross, the nature of our response to injustice might be the only thing which eventually leads to the exposure of such a culture and, in time, its redemption.

37. Wednesday

Watch therefore, and pray always

> trust me, Yorick, when to gratify a private appetite, it is once resolved upon, that an innocent and an helpless creature shall be sacrificed, 'tis an easy matter to pick up sticks enough from any thicket where it has strayed, to make a fire to offer it up with.

In writing about sacrifice Sterne is speaking about the destruction of reputation. He recognises the alacrity with which someone may be hounded and destroyed. When "fact-checking" was even more problematic than it is today, falsehoods could achieve a head-start that would be difficult to overtake. At one point, Sterne had to engage a friend to intercept and counter a rumour that he and his wife had entered a permanent separation. This was not only a matter of personal concern but, especially for her, a situation in which the ability to raise funds etc. would be compromised by any suggestion that the Sternes's marriage was in difficulty.

Laurence recognised in the world around him a gulf between the example of biblical discipleship and the sorry state of Christendom. Of the apostles: "Ye took up your crosses cheerfully, and followed him". In contrast, Sterne preached about "our cold and frozen affection" that "will part with nothing for his sake, not even our vices and follies". While many of the churchgoers in England today might look back into history for the comfort of a golden age of church attendance, Sterne preached about the "little stock of religion which is left". He knew, as did his congregation, that many factors influenced church attendance and some of them had very little to do with religious convictions.

In all of this Sterne is attempting to achieve a balance between his belief that most of us fail to live out the meaning and implications of faith, and his equally strong conviction that humanity is not intended to live out all its days in misery. Perhaps he is implying that meanness of spirit becomes both a bar to living out true religion and that, simultaneously, denies us the opportunity to experience a joyous celebration of life.

The degree to which Sterne suggests that he lived in an irreligious time can be gauged to some extent from within his preaching. He spoke about people who "got into the fashion of laughing at religion, and treating it with scorn and contempt". In the same sermon, he refers to the "languishing state of religion in the present age". Despite the presence of the church in every community, Sterne gives the impression that many people treated faith as a distant and irrelevant dimension of life:

> and, though one would expect, that at least the more
> solemn seasons of the year, set apart for the
> contemplation of Christ's sufferings, should give some
> check and interruption to them, yet what appearance is
> there ever amongst us, that it is so;- what one alteration
> does it make to the course of things?

Across many years, and in many churches, I have sat with people in Holy Week and reflected on what the events we remember might mean for us today. There can be an intensity, an immersion, in Christian spirituality at this time of the year which enables - momentarily - a focus on what we might call the primary questions of faith. From acclamation to desertion; from joy at supper with friends to the agony and suffering of what we will remember on Good Friday. Compressed into these few days are the meat and drink of the Christian faith.

In keeping with the theology and thought of his age, Sterne is deeply aware of the fragility of life and the judgement of God. As he puts it in his preaching: "We are standing upon the edge of a precipice, with nothing but the single thread of human life to hold us up". Taking the instruction of Jesus to his disciples in the Garden of Gethsemane, Sterne urges his hearers to "watch therefore, and pray always". In the fragility and uncertainty of life - of which he was intimately aware - Sterne urges people to be alert to getting lost in the follies of the world.

As we journey through Holy Week, when the action of Christ in washing the feet of the disciples is remembered, and the events are put in motion that led to his betrayal, it is fitting to ask: "what alteration does this make in our lives?"

38. Thursday

Everyone hates a tourist

I began my journey to ordained ministry in the 1980s. At that time the Church did not appear to favour younger candidates in the selection process. The clergy involved in supporting the exploration of my vocation placed considerable emphasis on gaining broader life experiences. This was all well and good, as far as it went, but care is needed to avoid a simplistic impression of other people's lives. It is wise to listen and learn - but foolish to think that a few months here or there teach us the full experience of someone else's life. Not least because our expectations about the future can be a powerful influence on our conception of the present.

I have long loved the Britpop track *Common People* by Pulp. The song narrates the desire of a rich young woman to experience the life of the poor. It is a vibrant and witty song, exposing the practice of "slumming" - basically, voyeurism of the poor. However, the lyric concludes that despite the wish to experience it, there is a fundamental flaw in her plan. The reason is that "If you called your dad he could stop it all". Possessing the possibility of escape or extraction is what is lacking from the lives of people who are poor. The lives of people struggling to survive are not temporary states that will suddenly be brought to an end. Perceptions of hope and a future - or the absence of them - are a critical part of what it means to be poor.

This paradox reminds me of an occasion when the Spanish owner of some rural holiday accommodation described the recent stay of some American tourists. At one point, as they worked out what they wanted to do, they asked the owner: "Can you take us where there are no tourists?" He couldn't help but comment that if he did that, then tourists would be present! However hard we might try, it is important to recognise the fundamental difference between the lives people are living, and the temporary tourism of those who have no idea about the interior experience of an alternative reality. Yes, things can be learned, but the differences should be recognised in all their depth, power and complexity.

Might this kind of charge be levelled at Jesus? At the start of Lent, we saw in the wilderness the devil presenting temptations to Jesus. If Jesus had accepted these temptations his mission would have ended before it had started. The incarnation is far more than divine tourism. It is an immersion in the reality of being human and, consequently, an event that removes the possibility of rescue by God, angels or any kind of super-human means. There is no escape route once the gift of incarnation has been made.

Throughout Lent, my reflection on Sterne has engaged with a persistent strand in his writing which relates to compassion. Compassion can be understood as the experience, as far as we are able to, of entering into the suffering of another. Unlike a tourist, passing through a country within a bubble of privilege, compassion can only be achieved when we recognise and understand our own vulnerabilities and needs. It is far more reciprocal in its nature than the passing observation of different lives. When Yorick encountered Father Lorenzo at Calais the interaction began with a judgemental observation on Parson Yorick's part but moved into a scene of genuine conversation. More than that, it evolved - through the exchange of gifts - into a significant silence:

> We remained silent, without any sensation of that foolish pain which takes place, when in such a circle you look for ten minutes in one another's faces without saying a word.

This absence of speech represents a moment of deep connection. While the time they spend together is very brief, it is of such consequence to Yorick that - having learned of Father Lorenzo's death - he takes the trouble to visit the grave and, there, "burst into a flood of tears".

Jesus was not a tourist, and we are not tourists. We live lives immersed in the changes and chances of a world (mostly) beyond our control. In Gethsemane, Jesus petitioned his father to take away from him the destiny that was unfolding. In due course, we shall all return home. For the present we are called to live in this world with compassion; mindful of our errors; and hopeful for what has been promised.

39. Good Friday

Infinite Labour

Good Friday was often the occasion for a charity sermon to be preached. On the 17th of April 1747, Sterne gave such a sermon at St Michael-Le-Belfrey, beside York Minster, in aid of two local charity schools. The service was attended by the Mayor and, subsequently, this became Sterne's first published sermon.

The financial nature of charity sermons, with organisers favouring preachers most able to prise open the purses of the wealthy, was not wholly to Sterne's liking. Nevertheless, the service raised a very respectable £62 (approximately £12,000 in today's terms). Sterne certainly appeared able and willing to press the cause for which he was speaking, emphasising the fundamental importance of access to education. However, his direction in the sermon has wider implications than simply shilling for shillings. The title of the sermon is "The Case of Elijah and the widow of Zerephath", with a verse taken from 1 Kings 17:16.

Several of the themes which have emerged during these reflections for Lent appear in this sermon. Not least of these is compassion. The context in which the narrative of this story is set involves both bereavement and famine. It is perhaps significant that Sterne makes the point, early in his sermon, that the widow had undoubtedly "fenced against this tragic event with all the thrifty management which self-preservation and parental love could inspire". In every society, there is a temptation to blame suffering upon those who suffer. It is the consolation of many in the middle classes that it is their prudence, hard work and foresight that has enabled them to evade poverty. By implication, others must have been less frugal and restrained. Many voices in society, not least in the tabloid press, promote a narrative of profligacy for those who seek support and aid from the wider community. To emphasise his belief in the prudence of the widow was to prevent easy access to our most common excuse of choice. "She brought it on herself".

On meeting the widow Elijah is told that she is about to make the last meal for herself and her son before they die. It is an affecting encounter. Elijah persists in asking for the first cake that she will make and assures her that neither the meal nor the oil will run out. Whether in resignation, conviction, doubt or faith, the widow agrees to his request. As Sterne reflects:

> Compassion is sometimes more than a balance for self-preservation.

It may seem odd that a prophet so capable of producing abundance should have been in such need when he met the widow. Perhaps it is the case that the encounter becomes the necessary catalyst for the miracle God is about to bestow. It is in the meeting of strangers, and the generosity of someone who had next to nothing, that the certainty of death is confounded.

As the biblical story unfolds, what had seemed a happy ending takes a dramatic turn. The woman's son becomes ill and dies. In response to her pleas, Elijah heals the child and returns him to his mother. She had thought him dead, but he is alive: lost to the world, but now found by Elijah and restored. Here, surely, is joy as great as that of the father embracing the Prodigal.

In the middle of his sermon, Sterne asks those present to imagine, for a moment, how his hearers would be if they lived up to the highest expectations of their faith "according to our conceptions of the deity". Sterne suggests that many of those present would conceive of this in the character of "a compassionate benefactor". In pressing the point, he begins to describe the greatest manifestation of this character, as someone "willing to undergo all kinds of affliction, to sacrifice himself, to forget his dearest interests, and even lay down his life". Instantly, we are back at Good Friday.

Sterne is preaching the God "who becamest poor, that we might be rich" - a figure without a place to call home; choosing to be "of no reputation"; taking the form of a servant; "led like a lamb to the slaughter". All of this constitutes what Sterne describes as "the infinite labour of this day's love".

Jesus does not arrive as some benevolent philanthropist intent on dolling out charity to the poor, the suffering and the unloved. Like Elijah he comes in need and begs our generosity, even when we feel that such sharing is beyond us, and little more than death awaits us. In the incarnation, God isn't a donor, but a participant. Many years ago, while studying sociology, I came across the dictum that "services for the poor become poor services". God does not supply services to the poor - God becomes poor. It is this complete identification, exemplified today by a God devoid of property, people and power, that is for Stene a "stupendous instance of compassion".

Tomorrow, emptiness might be the best description of the Church's life. In Tristram Shandy, Sterne inserted a blank page as a mischievous opportunity for the reader to draw one of the female characters as the reader imagined her. It is a startling reminder that when we read, in the mind's eye, we each imagine very different forms. For Sterne, this was also about the disparity between our reality, our longings and our hopes.

Perhaps tomorrow, the day of great absence, you might wish to ponder the blank page, using this moment between death and resurrection to consider, write or otherwise express, your desires.

40. Holy Saturday

Easter Day

The Lord is Risen

In northern Europe, in Medieval times, some priests marked the celebration of Easter by telling jokes from the pulpit. These could be risque and surprising (although many were probably very conventional) and sometimes slapstick humour was performed. The purpose was to produce laughter from the congregation. Laughter was seen as the most fitting way to mark the resurrection, the joke that we hear in the taunting words of St Paul: "Where, O death, is your victory? Where, O death, is your sting?" Death's smug certainty of our ending is overturned by the one who has walked out of the tomb.

Sterne was a passionate believer in humour and that life is infinitely duller without it. As we have seen, *Shandeanism* was intended to make us feel more alive, with humour running through our veins and giving energy to our spirits. Along with many other clergy of his day, Sterne would stand at the altar in Stillington, Sutton-on-the-Forest, or Coxwold and address the congregation in the words set out for Holy Communion in the Prayer Book: "Lift up your hearts".

If not with laughter, I often experience gladness and joy when Easter arrives. There is a kind of jest in the observation of early morning on Easter Day, when the world appears unchanged and pursuing its normal path. Yet to the eye of faith, this is the one day that changes all days - when the ordinary things of life become truly themselves, finding in the Risen Christ the life that will not die. This is expressed for me in the painting "Easter Morning" by Caspar David Friedrich. At first light, with the moon still in the sky, three figures appear to be walking down a country road. Nothing about the scene would tell you instantly that this is Easter morning. The title transforms the setting. Are these the women going to the tomb - or is it a later century, with worshippers making their way to an early service?

When Sterne wrote that he hoped his sermon would serve as a "flap upon the heart", he was thinking about the capacity of preaching to awaken conscience and compassion, encouraging charitable donations. Yet this image of stimulation suggests to me an act of resuscitation, with the heart requiring mirth and an occasional massage, in order to clear blockages and spiritual malaise. In this sense, across both his lively fiction and his impassioned sermons, Sterne is performing CPR* for the soul. On Easter Day we are jolted once again to greet our improbable saviour and to embrace that joy which is only a foretaste of our heavenly home. That bright pavilion lit with sacred fire, in which there is heavenly riot and festivity.

*   Cardiopulmonary resuscitation

Afterword

Recovering Wit

Deadpan sarcasm and satire can be one of the highest forms of humour. Religious humour can be one of the wisest means of conveying God's truth. Sharp truths can pierce the conscience to the soul. It can get to the heart of the matter. It can make us laugh at ourselves and see us as God sees us. Otherwise, we might just cry. But is humour the proper work of God, and can something like Laurence Sterne's writings ever be proper material for a devotional study, let alone in a season of sobriety such as Lent?

The answer must be 'yes' since Sterne's literary corpus represents a remarkable form of *Implicit Religion* – a term coined by the late Edward Bailey, also a clergyman, and an accomplished sociologist. In common with other kinds of sociological outlooks, Bailey regarded Implicit Religion as a 'take' on life itself; a way of viewing the apparently ordinary and familiar. Implicit Religion is not like the lens of 'Folk Religion', which looks at specific acts of communal and individual spirituality that are largely outside the control of mainstream 'religious' activity. Nor is Implicit Religion an approach comparable to the fields of 'civil' or 'folk' in outlook. Rather, Implicit Religion is the intentional and intense focus on ordinary everyday activity that may appear, at first sight, to possess no element of spirituality or religion at all. Moreover, participants may have no explicit idea that what they are doing can be read and understood as 'religious'. So, their participation is often unconscious. Or, as Bailey would maintain, a matter of Implicit Religion.

Thus, the concept of Implicit Religion can counter the tendency to automatically equate 'religion' with specialised institutions, articulated beliefs, and specific religious behaviour. Above all, the lens of Implicit Religion allows us to read aspects of contemporary society for elements of religiosity within what might conventionally be seen as a 'normative' secular sphere to the more casual observer.

It is this approach that Chris Swift has skilfully brought to his treatment of Laurance Sterne, and it is entirely complementary, insofar as Sterne himself took everyday life seriously, and used humour to shine a light on the Church of England at the time, which had become self-enclosed and evolved into an oblivious form of polity. Sterne saw faith alive in the world – the secular domain. And Sterne saw secularism – grasping ambition and pomposity that needed satire to burst the ecclesiastical bubble of the established church – alive and well in the Church of England.

The whole approach adopted by Implicit Religion flips equations and turns the normal ways of reading faith and life upside down. Once one begins to appreciate how spiritual Sterne's sarcasm and satire actually were, the avenues for a new understanding of devotional approaches to seasons such as Lent start to open up.

For some readers, it may come as a surprise that the term 'secularisation' is not secular in origin. The word is derived from *saeculum* and refers to our time, age, generation or century. No less a surprise is that the term 'religion' is not religious in origin either. From the Latin word *religare*, it means to bind things together. Ancient sources were, if anything, quite banal in what they regarded as secular, and the term was often used to describe inanimate moveable objects, such as furniture. These were, after all, things of their time and place, and they belonged to an age. They were temporal. On the other hand, the religious were bound together and referred to that which endured beyond us.

The notion of 'secular priests' in medieval Europe made perfect sense. These clergy belonged to the world and were not part of an enclosed order. Secular clergy were moveable, living off the tithes and offerings the people provided. Monks who were temporarily released from their cloisters were *exclaustration – literally lived "beyond the walls" of their enclosure for a season.*

Throughout the New Testament, the secular realm simply means the current age, with its rulers and laws. It is not anti-religious, as though it was somehow in opposition to a theocracy. The secular world contained every shade of the good, bad and ugly, and was always a fusion of divine and human. Thus, we find Jesus commending the shrewd 'children of this age' (*saeculum* – Luke 16). But this does not prohibit Jesus from also commending the 'children of light' who belong to the age that is to come. The Christian worldview was inevitably flecked with temporal pragmatism. 'Render unto Caesar what is Caesar's and to God what belongs to God' (Mark 12:17) was a typical dictum.

Christians have to balance their inherent dual citizenship. They belong to their own place, space and time, and are to be good model citizens wherever they are. At the same time, they owe allegiances that are supra-spatial, and in terms of values and devotion, eternal. They live in the world but are not of the world.

In ancient thinking, few would have assumed this constituted a tension that needed to be resolved. The secular realm had its own logic, values and rationality. Likewise, the sacred, or religious realm, was rooted in the wisdom of God, belonging to an age to come. A world turned upside down, in which earthly hierarchies would be inverted. The first would be last, and the last first.

Pollsters tell us that fewer and fewer people today are religious, but at the same time, they are not necessarily secular – at least in the modern sense of that term. The emerging generation is often characterised by sociologists and researchers as 'spiritual-but-not-religious' (SBNRs) – or 'nones'. That is to say, they are intuitively inclined to the sacred and enchantment but not minded to express their spiritual inklings in any form of religious commitment or belonging.

In many respects, this is more of an ancient phenomenon than a modern one. The secular-religious divide that has characterised modernity is rapidly disintegrating, with a more spiritually diffuse postmodern age emerging in its place. For 'nones', commitments to fairness, justice, values, causes, campaigns, eco-concerns, climate change, tolerance and spirituality are core.

Institutional religion has been caught napping, failing to read the signs of the times. Our forebears had no difficulty knowing and encountering the reality of God in the secular realm. That is the realm that all must inhabit. The sacred or religious sphere was merely a small, protected enclave with its own discrete culture and laws. At that time, few lived within its confines, let alone prepared to wholly subject themselves to its rule.

The more churches retreat from the secular world, the more sectarian they become. As countries behind the Iron Curtain discovered, erecting walls and devising systems to keep the people inside 'safe' from external influence only led to a citizenry of begrudging compliance. Escapees and defectors increased, whilst incomers were rare.

'Nones' do not see the world in terms of secular-scared division. Their spiritual geography is more like the proverbial African farm. There is no fence or wall. The only question relates to how far you are from the farmhouse and in which direction you are walking. There is no fence to mark insiders from outsiders. On such ground – the vast plain of the secular – churches must meet the 'children of this age'.

The emerging generation is disinclined to opt out of a world where they can readily encounter God beyond the confines of organised religion. The children of this age have discovered that the secular is saturated with signs of the sacred, pulsating with signals of transcendence and enduring spiritual enchantment. So, it would seem that just as we can find God in wisdom, so can we also discern the work of the Spirit in wit, satire and sharp, scathing humour. There is such a thing as Holy Wit to cultivate too – which is not collecting bad jokes. Rather, it is knowing God works through subversion, humour, laughter and playful irony.

According to one 20th-century mystic-theologian, 'heaven is a laugh freed forever'. We can make two observations in closing since heaven came to earth in Jesus. We may well discern the Spirit at work in humour. But equally, the Spirit will discern us in humour, and that is the more profound work of God. Honest, that is no joke.

The Very Revd Professor Martyn Percy